The Spirit-filled Steward

The Spirit-filled Steward

Charles McKay

Convention Press/Nashville, Tennessee

5131–07

Church Services and Materials Division
Allen B. Comish, Director
Code number: Church Study Course
This book is the text for course
3107 of subject area 31, Christian
Growth and Service, of the Church
Study Course.

Dewey Decimal Classification: 248.1
Printed in the United States of America

To my four grandchildren
Ernie, Jr. and Kay Myers
Lanell and Lisa Wood

Foreword

If an association test were given to Baptists, it has been speculated that 95 percent of them would think of the word "money" upon hearing the word "stewardship." The giving of money to God is a part of stewardship, but this is by no means all of it.

Being bolder in the use of "stewardship" than "money," Baptists have tended to downgrade the "other than money" meaning of stewardship.

Dr. Charles L. McKay in this book has given us a valid departure point for man's response to God's salvation through Christ Jesus—stewardship. He helps us see various aspects of stewardship as they relate to the Christian and the Christian life. The life of the mature steward is the Spirit-filled life.

Bedrock, scriptural, and spiritual motivation for Christian living and service is to be found in the complete understanding of what it means to be a steward. Dr. McKay has presented in this book a comprehensive treatment of what my Bible professor, Dr. O. W. Yates, used to distill in a few words, "When you warm a man's heart, you warm his pocketbook." When the mind is informed and the heart is warmed, stewardship of money will be positionized properly.

This is a basic book, a primer in stewardship. However, at any point in the Christian's journey he will find in this book Bible-based guidance and inspiration for living the Spirit-filled life of a Christian steward.

E. Stanley Williamson
Director of Stewardship Development
Stewardship Commission
Southern Baptist Convention

Contents

About the Author

 Charles L. McKay, pastor of the First Southern Baptist Church of Scottsdale, Arizona, has been a pastor for more than twenty years. He also has served churches in Mississippi, Louisiana, and Alabama.

Dr. McKay served for fourteen years as executive secretary-treasurer of the Arizona Southern Baptist Convention. Under his leadership the convention more than doubled in size.

Before going to Arizona, Dr. McKay was for five years director of enlargement and evangelism in the Sunday School Department of the Sunday School Board.

This is Dr. McKay's fifth book.

Introduction

There is an urgent need today for deep searching into the meaning of complete stewardship. Nominal Christianity is a peril to today's church. If allowed to continue, it will reduce the testimony of the church to a whisper. The aim of this book is to point the way to a happy, dynamic, Spirit-filled, and useful life for the cause of Christ. It will challenge Christians to a much higher and more complete stewardship than the stewardship of money.

Christianity is not simply an invitation to accept divine love. It calls on believers to demonstrate that love. The test of a good steward is whether he loves God and others in the same manner that he loves himself. Love that seeks the best for others is stewardship at its best.

The Christian enterprise has suffered because of our failure to present a total biblical stewardship. Many church members have never faced total stewardship at all. Some have considered only certain aspects of it. Too many have identified stewardship only with the giving of money—the tithe or some other percentage. Too many church members are ignorant of complete biblical stewardship—its basis, meaning, practice, and results.

Stewardship is as comprehensive as life itself. This book will present the claims of our Lord upon man—all that he is, has, and can become—

after he responds to God's call to salvation and accepts the free offer of redemption. Further, it will set forth the redeemed man's obligation to a total commitment to the lordship of Jesus Christ and to the will of God for his life. In doing this, the believer dethrones himself and enthrones Jesus Christ. It is then that the Holy Spirit gains complete control of a life.

At conversion the Holy Spirit enters the believer, never to leave the redeemed possession (Eph. 1:13–14). He is the earnest, or partial down payment, for the possession. As a redeemed man yields to him, the indwelling and empowering Holy Spirit takes over the controls of his life. As the Christian grows in grace, he accepts his stewardship obligation and privileges as the will of his Master. Christians must be taught much of this obligation. This book is an attempt to offer a growing segment of Christians adequate information concerning Christian stewardship.

Too long people have been left with the impression that giving is all there is to stewardship. When a Christian becomes aware of the presence, purpose, and power of the Holy Spirit in his life, he will begin to grow toward his potential and will begin to discover and practice the joys of complete stewardship. One of the side effects of total stewardship may be that it will become unnecessary to spend much time on the small segment of stewardship involving money.

It is the sincere prayer of the author that this book may lead many to dedicate their talents, time, substance, self, and all else they are to the lordship of Jesus Christ. In such may Christ be magnified, God our Father glorified, and the Holy Spirit pleased.

Charles L. McKay

1 Your Christian Life Is on Display

"Wherefore seeing we also are compassed about with so great a cloud of witnesses, let us lay aside every weight, and the sin which doth so easily beset us, and let us run with patience the race that is set before us, looking unto Jesus the author and finisher of our faith; who for the joy that was set before him endured the cross, despising the shame, and is set down at the right hand of the throne of God" (*Heb. 12:1–2*).

Christians attended the arena in the first centuries, but often they were there to be living prey for wild beasts. Often they were chosen because of their faith in and loyalty to Jesus Christ their Lord.

The scene referred to in Hebrews 12:1–2 was quite different. The writer to the Hebrews knew that those to whom he wrote were aware of the exciting races in the coliseum. In some cities the wide roadway between the coliseum and the temple was decorated on both sides with bronze busts and plaques of champions. The ambition of every contestant was to have his name written on one of those plaques.

The writer of Hebrews was thinking of a race of far more importance; and the place for the names of the runners had far greater significance: the Lamb's Book of Life. The emphasis is not on winning; the emphasis is on the stewardship of running a worthy race. Since every Christian runs this race, the list of spectators is offered for encouragement and inspiration. To run well and with patience is the goal. Others, not in the heavenly bleachers, but in our neighborhood, and wherever we travel, will notice also how well we run. Our seriousness and concern for how well we run may well provide others a measure by which they judge their need and response to Christ.

Compare the Two Races

1. Both Races Have Spectators

Spectators in Olympian and Corinthian races came to watch the race. Hebrews 11 is filled with the names of God's faithful who have died, holding on to their faith in him. These are called "a cloud of witnesses." They are God's "hall of fame."

After listing these names, the writer said, "Time would fail me to tell of" all of the spectators (Heb. 11:32). Those who run in the Christian race must remember that members of his personal family, his church family, and his community are watching this race. They will see how well the race is run.

2. Both Races Have Strong Motivation

The runner in both races has at least four strong motivating factors. First, earthly and heavenly spectators are watching and he desires to do well. Second, the race is worthwhile because the goal is good. Third, the goal is to gain the presence of the race's sponsor. And finally,

16

others have done it, so can you. For the Christian there is strength in knowing that nothing could stop the victory of Jesus Christ over the worst obstacles Satan could offer.

3. Both Races Require Discipline and Training

Those who would run well in either race must resolve, "This *one* thing I do" (Phil. 3:13). Both races demand self-discipline, the whole person brought under the control of a great purpose. The discipline and training that one is willing to undergo is determined by his dedication to the task and the value he puts on reaching the goal, facing the referee (judge), and the effect of his race on the spectators. There are some do's and dont's for those who desire to run well. A runner must stay within the limits of the raceway. A wise runner does not look back, for it will cost him momentum, distract him, jeopardize his balance and rhythm, cause him to collide with other runners, and cause him to lose sight of the goal. A wise runner keeps a rhythmic pace, with smooth, natural, and even strides. A wise runner budgets his strength, saving some effort for the last part of the race. A wise runner carries as little extra weight as possible. All of these are applicable to both races and call for extra effort and discipline by the participant. All must run (live), yet some are not willing to pay the price to run well. Some are satisfied with less than a good effort. Some are searching for a better way to run (live).

Self-denial is essential if an athlete is to do his best. Jesus says to those who would run the Christian race well, "Deny yourself, take up the cross daily, and follow me" (Matt. 16:24, author's translation). To Jesus, his cross means death. When he says "cross," he means nothing less than death to self. The Christian is to reckon

17

himself dead, but alive (Rom. 6:11). Paul said, "If Christ be in you, the body is dead because of sin; but the Spirit is life because of righteousness" (Rom. 8:10).

In life's race, God does not require that his redeemed meet life's standards of success, but they are to be faithful.

4. Both Races Have Starting Points

In Olympian races, runners must abide by the rules set forth by the officials. For the race of life, Jesus Christ drew up the rules and limits. He outlined the qualifications and the regulations. He made the plan for beginning the Christain race simple enough that everyone who feels accountable to God for his sins could understand it.

The Bible teaches, "All have sinned, and come short of the glory of God" (Rom. 3:23). "There is none righteous, no, not one" (Rom. 3:10). Everyone must accept this fact. Further, the Bible teaches, "Except ye repent, ye shall all likewise perish" (Luke 13:3,5). It is not enough to repent of sin. After one repents of his sin he should then believe on the Lord Jesus Christ, for it is then that Christ becomes Lord and Savior.

The beginning of the Christian life is at the point of personal faith in Jesus Christ as Lord and Savior. To Nicodemus, Jesus described the starting point in the Christian life in these words: "For God so loved the world, that he gave his only begotten Son, that whosoever believeth in him should not perish, but have everlasting life" (John 3:16).

5. Only One of the Races Has Practice Runs

Before the runner enters the arena at the coliseum, he endures hours of disciplined practice and rigid training. Long before he is allowed to go before the spectators to perform, he has made a good preparation for the exhibition. This is not so with the Christian. He is observed carefully by the spectators from the moment he becomes a contestant in the race. He has no time to practice. There are no training sessions before he enters the arena. The race is on the minute he professes his faith in Jesus Christ.

6. Both Races Have a Judge

Only one can win in the Olympian race, and the judge decides the winner. In the Christian arena everyone who enters this race on Christ's terms will be a winner. The Judge of men and life will reveal from the records how well each man has done.

Motivation for the Christian Race

1. Those in the Grandstand

The Bible calls attention to the witnesses watching the race. Any coach knows that athletes seldom do their best in practice. Records are broken in competition. The athlete's reputation is at stake; spectators are counting on him to do his best. He must not disappoint friends and fans. The Christian has watching him a great cloud of witnesses already in heaven as well as living loved ones and friends. He is a public spectacle, on display. This is a challenge to do his best. His Lord also looks on.

2. The Victor's Crown

Nothing can challenge faithfulness like the author and finisher of our faith, Jesus. At the finish line stands our Lord and Savior, waiting to place upon each one the laurel of victory. Paul expressed it in these words: "For I am now ready to be offered, and the time of my departure is at hand. I have fought a good fight, I have finished my course, I have kept the faith: henceforth there is laid up for me a crown of righ-

teousness, which the Lord, the righteous judge,
shall give me at that day: and not to me only,
but unto all them also that love his appearing"
(2 Tim. 4:6–8).

An Urgent Appeal to Those in the Race
1. Lay Aside Every Weight
I never shall forget one basketball team that
came to our school to play. These tall giants,
who made our players look like grasshoppers,
came on the floor to warm up with heavy shackles
around their ankles. They had to hobble around
to warm up because of the weights on their legs.
But when the signal was given to begin the game,
the coach cried out, "Shackles off, boys!" and
the weights were removed. I had never before
seen men so swift and light-footed as those
opponents.

The writer to the Hebrews called to every
runner in the Christian race to "unshackle." Do
not let your race be handicapped by some unnecessary ball and chain. Too many Christians
are bound. Their progress in the Christian life
is not what it could be, because of unnecessary
extras that hinder them. The runners in an
Olympian race would not dare enter the arena
with shackles and attempt to run. How much
more important it is for Christians, who are
always on exhibition before a great cloud of
witnesses, to lay aside every weight.

2. And the Sin That Does So Easily Beset Us
The writer of Hebrews, guided by the Holy
Spirit, warned Christians to put aside "the sin
which doth so easily beset us" (Heb. 12:1).

As a nine-year-old, I ran the fifty-yard dash
with some of my schoolmates. For the first half
of the race I was in the lead. But I lost the race.
In making my track shorts, my dear mother had

attached some straps that went over my shoulders. These suspenders had me occupied by keeping them up and in place on my shoulders, and some of my opponents passed me by.

An athlete must be careful about the garb he wears. It can help or hinder. Christians must "lay aside every weight, and the sin which doth so easily beset us."

3. Let Us Run

A racehorse is trained to run. A ballplayer contributes most, not on the bench, but in the game doing his best. A doctor is where he is needed when he is attending his patient. A teacher is at his best when he is in the classroom teaching. A Christian in the race of life is to run until he crosses the finish line.

4. With Patience

Almost everyone who exercises regularly speaks of the boredom of exercising alone. To keep up a regular discipline of exercise, or Christian living, requires the development of the skill of patience. The race can be finished only by taking one step at a time. Life is lived one day at a time, and strength is given as it is called for. In the Sermon on the Mount, Jesus warned against the anxiety over the future which makes one miss the present.

5. Looking to Jesus

Jesus is the author of and completes our faith. While dying at the hands of those who stoned him to death, Stephen, the first Christian martyr, was looking unto Jesus, the author and finisher of his faith. As Stephen bore witness to his faith, Jesus stood at the right hand of the Father with the challenge for Stephen to finish the last lap of the race and receive his crown.

Isaiah was looking unto the Lord when he saw him high and lifted up, his train filling the Temple. When John was in prison on the Isle of Patmos, he was in the Spirit on the Lord's Day when Jesus revealed himself. A door was opened in heaven, and John saw "a throne set" and on it Jesus, the King of kings. While John looked upon Jesus, the King of kings, he realized that the Roman Emperor was not the ruler of the universe.

Men who look upon Jesus exclaim with the officers, "Never man spake like this man" (John 7:46). With John the Baptist we cry out to others, "Behold the Lamb of God, which taketh away the sins of the world" (John 1:29).

2 God's Plan Is for You; Accept It

"Jesus saith unto them, My meat is to do the will of him that sent me, and to finish his work" (John 4:34).

God follows a plan in doing his work both in heaven and on earth. He has a blueprint for each life. Jesus said, "Whosoever shall do the will of God, the same is my brother, and my sister, and mother" (Mark 3:35). Jesus taught that every man had his own work. Not to every man some plan, but to every man God's plan for every life. Jesus said, "I must work the works of him that sent me, while it is day: the night cometh, when no man can work" (John 9:4). Again he said, "To this end was I born, and for this cause came I into the world" (John 18:37).

"I raised thee up [Pharaoh], that I might

shew my power in thee, and that my name might be declared throughout all the earth" (Rom. 9:17). Who knows but that if Pharaoh had followed God's plan for his life, he might have been a mighty force for righteousness like Elijah or Moses or David? God raised up Pharaoh that he might show his (God's) power and declare his name through him in all the earth. Pharaoh failed to accept God's plan for his life. It would be difficult to believe that God planned the tragic life of Pharaoh.

Joseph said to his brothers, "Ye thought evil against me; but God meant it unto good" (Gen. 50:20). God had a plan for Joseph. He had a plan for Pharaoh. He has a plan for everyone.

On one occasion the sons of God presented themselves before the Lord. The devil also presented himself. God said to the devil: "Have you considered my servant Job? Try him out, consider him, sift him in the sieve of Satan and see what you find in a man that has accepted completely God's plan for his life." (See Job 1:8–12.) God used Job as an example to prove that one who follows God's plan completely will be rewarded, and will be empowered by the Holy Spirit to remain true to God if he so desires.

When God spoke to Abraham in Ur of the Chaldees, he did not tell Abraham what he had in mind for him. He said, "Get thee out of thy country, and from thy kindred" (Gen. 12:1), and Abraham started following God's will for his life. Step by step, God revealed his plan to Abraham. He did not lay the entire plan down like a map before him. He did not let Abraham know at the beginning what the outcome might be. "Just follow me," said God, and Abraham followed. Abraham did not have to follow, but he did. He accepted God's will for his life. He never regretted the decision.

Many women wonder what part they have in God's great program. They have the responsibility of the children. They must handle the affairs at home. They wonder if God uses them in his plan. God has a plan for each woman's life.

A baby was born to a Jewish woman. She saw that he was a goodly child. She kept him hidden as long as possible. She then took some sticks, pitch, and slime and made a little cradle-like boat. Tenderly she placed the baby Moses in the little cradle-like boat. God had a plan for Moses' sister. Suppose that she had failed God. Just a little girl—suppose she had not done what God wanted her to do. God would have had to use another to work out his plan and purpose for Moses to be spared for the great work he had for him.

After Pharaoh's daughter found Moses, this little sister begged the daughter of Pharaoh to let her mother (his own) take care of him. Knowing that she would have him for only a few years in her home, Moses' mother knew she must do her best for God. She instilled in Moses' heart God's love, God's program, and God's will for his life. Who had the greater part in doing God's will, Moses, his sister, or his mother? God has a plan for every life, and one life is as important as another. Have you found his plan for your life?

Men wonder what part they can play in God's great program for his church and his missionary cause. God has a plan for you. God will use you. Think of Moses on the mountainside. As long as he held his arms upward toward heaven, the victory was Israel's. But his hands got heavy; and when he let them drop to his side, the enemy prevailed. Aaron and Hur committed their hands to hold up the hands of Moses. They found a rock and Moses sat on it. Aaron held up one hand of Moses to heaven and Hur held up the other, and the army of God prevailed against the enemy.

Man, no matter who or where you are, stay by your church, by your pastor, by the leaders, and by the work of God, and do what God gives you to do. God's plan for you is as essential as it is for the preacher or the singer or anyone else. God has a plan for us. He will use us if we let him.

Two hundred faint men in David's army were unable to cross the brook to pursue the enemy. Four hundred said, "We are well able"; they crossed the brook to pursue the enemy. After they had overtaken the enemy and returned with the spoils, some of the men said, "We'll keep the spoils for ourselves." David said: "Not so. You brave four hundred were well able to go. You went, but these two hundred did as much; they stayed by the stuff. We shall all share alike." (See 1 Sam. 30:23–24.)

God has no big places and little places in his service. It is as important to fill the pew as it is to stand in the pulpit if that is what God wants you to do, if that is his plan for your life.

When David was following the flock in the Judean hills, he had not dreamed that God had a plan for his life. He did not know that one day he would go to the king's palace, but David knew that he could watch his father's flock. He always did the best he knew how. Years later God crowned him with victories and successes.

It was hard when Joseph was denied the pleasures of home, or when he was abused by his brothers as they dropped him into the pit, or when he was sold to the merchants on their

way to Egypt, or when he was tricked by Poti-
phar's wife. It was hard for him, but evidently
he said, "This is God's will for my life." Then
one day he could say to his brothers who had
sold him, "You intended it for evil, but God
intended it for good." (See Gen. 50:20.) Joseph
had accepted God's plan for his life, and he was
willing to follow it at all costs.

One May Reject God's Plan for His Life

You may reject the plan of God for your life.
You may fail to follow the program God has
mapped out for you. You may completely reject
it. God allows it.

The psalmist said that created things are doing
God's will. The stars do what God wants stars
to do. The moon always does what God intended
the moon to do. The sun always does God's will.
Man alone is given the right of choice. He may
accept God's plan or reject it (Ps. 8).

God has given man the freedom of choice. God
would have used Pharaoh as an ambassador to
deliver his name to the nations of the earth, but
he failed God. He failed to surrender his stubborn
will to God's plan for his life.

God failed to get a favorable response from
Pharaoh. God gave him a dozen chances, but he
rejected them. Finally God hardened his heart
and helped Pharaoh do the thing he was bent on
doing. God never hardens a heart that has not
turned against him already.

The Price for Rejecting God's Will

Jezebel, a woman who had every chance to
become a great power and influence for God,
was the wife of a king. She had Elijah for a
preacher.

Jezebel decided that no plan of God would

27

fit her life. She refused God's will. She went to the depths of rebellion, finally to be overtaken by the judgment of God. That awful hour had been foretold by the prophets.

Jezebel fixed her hair, "made up" her face, and looked out the window to see the warrior Jehu coming. Jehu rode up and called out, "If there are any up there on my side, throw her out." The cries and screams of the queen as she was thrown from the window echoed in the streets. Her body hit the street, and the horses trampled her to death. (See 2 Kings 9:30–37.)

The men of war went to a banquet. There Jehu said: "That woman was the wife of a king; she was also the daughter of a king. We'll give her a burial." But few of Jezebel's remains could be found. The man or woman who rejects God's plan for his life will pay for it.

Jonah was determined not to do what God wanted him to do. God wanted him to go to Nineveh, but Jonah said, "I will not go." Instead, he sailed in another direction. A storm came, Jonah was pitched overboard, and a great fish swallowed him. After staying in the belly of the fish three days and nights, Jonah surrendered. He called out to God for mercy.

God sent wise men to Herod to tell that a newborn king, the Christ child, had come. Herod refused God's announcement. Lot was one of the great tragedies of homelife. He was a failure as a father and as a husband. His home went on the rocks. As a leader he failed. He rejected God's will.

The Rewards for Following God's Will

"By faith Moses, when he was come to years, refused to be called the son of Pharaoh's daughter; choosing rather to suffer affliction with the people of God, than to enjoy the pleasures of sin for a season; esteeming the reproach of Christ greater riches than the treasures in Egypt: for he had respect unto the recompense of the reward" (Heb. 11:24–26). Moses knew what he was turning down. He had offered to him the highest social and political position in Egypt. But Moses was looking forward to another reward. He knew that God had a blueprint for his life, and that blueprint did not include being a king of Egypt.

As some count success, Moses was a failure. He led the people of Israel forty years, but he never led them into the Promised Land. Moses went on to heaven instead of going to the Promised Land. Was Moses there enjoying heaven when God sent the heavenly choir to the Judean hills to sing of peace on earth, goodwill toward men? Was Moses looking on from the portals of glory when the babe was born in Bethlehem? When God sent two back to earth to talk to Jesus on the mount of transfiguration, he sent Moses and Elijah. Is it any wonder that Moses refused the riches of Egypt in order to identify himself with God's people?

God Offers Another Chance

God gives other chances to those who reject his will. Israel had marred God's plan, had followed other gods. God sent Jeremiah down to the potter's house. Jeremiah saw the potter take a piece of clay and try to mold it over the wheel into a vessel. As Jeremiah observed, the clay did not respond to the skilled potter. The clay was marred in his hand, and the vessel was not made. Jeremiah thought the potter would throw away the clay, but he did not. With all his skill, the potter took the piece of clay and on

29

another wheel shaped it into a beautiful vessel.

God gave Jonah another chance. Out of the belly of the whale Jonah cried to God, and God answered. God delivered him and gave him another chance.

God gave Samson other chances, and Samson took them. God gave Pharaoh a dozen chances, and he refused them all. He gave Simon Peter other chances. Peter accepted them and lived his life in the will of God.

It is glorious that God offers men second chances. He says, "Come unto me, all ye that labour and are heavy laden, and I will give you rest" (Matt. 11:28). He says, "Whosoever will, let him take the water of life freely" (Rev. 22:17). He says, "I have no pleasure in the death of the wicked . . . turn ye, turn ye . . . for why will ye die" (Ezek. 33:11).

How does one find God's will for his life? First, do the first thing that you know God wants you to do. Then he will reveal the second thing to you. Some people want to know all of God's will before deciding whether to accept it or not. God did not reveal everything to Saul of Tarsus on the Damascus road. When Saul asked, "What wilt thou have me to do?" God did not tell him everything; he only described the first step. (See Acts 9:6.) If Saul had not done the first thing Christ told him to do, he never would have found God's will.

Jesus said, "Except ye repent, ye shall . . . perish" (Luke 13:5). God's will is that unsaved sinners repent of sin. Then Christ saves. Those who have taken the first step should read God's Word, seek his will for their lives, and begin living for him. God rewards those who pray earnestly for guidance. The Spirit will guide into all truth. The believer becomes the Spirit's property at conversion. The Holy Spirit knows every step of God's will for every believer.

If you are not a child of God, believe on the Lord Jesus Christ and you shall be saved. If you are a child of God and have not found God's will for your life, pray the Spirit to guide you.

3 Your Duty to God and Country

"Render therefore unto Caesar the things which are Caesar's; and unto God the things that are God's" (Matt. 22:21).

Christian citizens have a twofold duty, one to their country and one to God. One who enjoys the rights and benefits of citizenship must accept responsibility as a citizen. Skills and money are needed to maintain a nation. The kingdom of God also must have committed men and money to operate. One who shares the rights and benefits of a citizen of the kingdom of God must bear responsibility as a citizen of that kingdom.

That Which Belongs to Caesar Should Be Returned to Him

1. Taxes Belong to Caesar

The word "render" means to return to Caesar

that which is his (Matt. 22:21). A citizen has certain obligations to his country. Citizenship also provides privileges. The rights and benefits of citizenship in the United States are many. These privileges never should be taken for granted.

2. Citizenship Imposes Obligations

The rights and benefits of citizenship cost something. This is the greatest place on earth to us, but it costs time, effort, and money to keep it that way. Those who enjoy the privileges should share the obligations. The state is justified, therefore, in asking citizens to share in the effort and expense. This one does by paying taxes and rendering service. Jesus said, "Render therefore unto Caesar the things which are Caesar's; and unto God the things that are God's" (Matt. 22:21).

Good citizens will support and defend their nation with their time, talent, energy, and possessions. One who does not pay his legal taxes is not a good citizen.

That Which Belongs to God Should be Returned to Him

Christian citizenship is twofold. An American who is a Christian is a citizen of a great country and also a citizen of a great kingdom. Therefore, he supports not only the state and the nation but the kingdom of God as well.

1. Everything We Possess Belongs to God

God owns everything by creation. "In the beginning God created the heaven and the earth" (Gen. 1:1). The earth is God's by right of creation. He made it; it belongs to him.

The earth is the Lord's, but that is not all. "The earth is the Lord's, and the fulness thereof; the world, and they that dwell therein" (Ps.

24:1). John said, "Without him was not any thing made that was made" (John 1:3). The psalmist tells us that if we have animals of any kind, they belong to God. God said, "Every beast of the forest is mine" (Ps. 50:10).

Further, God tells his people, "The silver is mine, and the gold is mine, saith the Lord of hosts" (Hag. 2:8). The money in your pocket, as well as your time and talents, belongs to God. "What hast thou that thou didst not receive?" (1 Cor. 4:7). We have received everything that we are and have in our possession.

God says, "We brought nothing into this world, and it is certain we can carry nothing out" (1 Tim. 6:7). Grave clothes have no pockets. "Lay up for yourselves treasures in heaven, where neither moth nor rust doth corrupt, and where thieves do not break through nor steal" (Matt. 6:20). Friends will not put many worthwhile possessions in the casket with our bodies. Heavenly treasures in time, service, and talents must be stored in advance. God owns everything. He permits us to lay up these treasures in heaven.

When Israel was about to enter the Promised Land, God warned them not to forget that he was their source of power to get wealth (Deut. 8:18). If you have money or other valuables, thank God for them. People who are blessed with this world's possessions should give God the glory, for the Bible teaches that God is the giver of wealth.

In this life, God expects his children to be good stewards. In the end all returns to him, for he is the owner of all. Jesus said of the rich fool, "This night thy soul shall be required of thee: then whose shall those things be?" (Luke 12:20).

2. Christians Belong to God by Redemption

Christians are bought and redeemed by the

blood of Jesus Christ. "While we were yet sinners, Christ died for us" (Rom. 5:8). We are
his because he made us. More than that, we are
his because he redeemed us. It was not with
corruptible things such as silver and gold but
with the precious blood of Jesus Christ that we
were redeemed. We belong to God. There never
should be any question with the Christian as to
his responsibility to God.

The heavenly Father can say to those who
are redeemed, "You are mine because I made
you, and you are mine because I redeemed you."
This is true because "God so loved the world,
that he gave his only begotten Son, that whosoever believeth in him should not perish, but
have everlasting life" (John 3:16). What a
price God paid for our redemption! We are his;
he made us; and while we were yet siners, Christ
died for us.

3. Christians Belong to God by Choice

God never has forced anyone to believe on his
Son. He says, "Come unto me, all ye that labour
and are heavy laden, and I will give you rest"
(Matt. 11:28). When the Holy Spirit calls and
the individual responds, God brings peace. Jesus
calls, the Holy Spirit convicts, but sinners must
repent and accept God's salvation by faith in
Jesus Christ. This must be the choice of the
sinner.

4. Christians Belong to God by Preservation

God keeps his children. It is not left to our
ability. Our Savior has sealed our salvation. Jesus
tells us that no man can pluck us from his
Father's hand. Paul emphatically said, "Being
confident of this very thing, that he which hath
begun a good work in you will perform it until
the day of Jesus Christ" (Phil. 1:6). "For it
is God which worketh in you both to will and

to do of his good pleasure" (Phil. 2:13). It is wonderful to belong to God and to be in his sustaining care. It is a blessed privilege to render unto God that which is his. The Macedonian Christians should be an example to us. It was said of them, "First they gave themselves to the Lord" (2 Cor. 8:5, RSV). Who can do less?

Partnership Between God and Man

1. Partnership Requires Sharing

Man is a steward, and it is required of a steward that he be found faithful (1 Cor. 4:2). When Jesus Christ returns to earth, he will have all stewards give account of themselves. We will have to acknowledge whether we have been faithful. When one accepts the ownership of God and the stewardship of man, he becomes a partner with God. To accept partnership with God is a glorious relationship.

If I had the privilege of building a thousand homes, I would build them all with Jesus as my partner. On April 14, 1928, my wife and I started our home. Both of us realized that without Jesus Christ we would fail. It was our desire to be partners with him who never fails. We asked Jesus our Savior to be our partner, to bless our home, to guide our lives, and to use us and what we had for his glory. These have been glorious, happy years. With God as our partner, they could not be otherwise.

2. Partnership Imposes Responsibility

For Christ to be our partner, we realized there would be responsibilities and obligations on our part. We promised him that if he would be our partner in our home, we would always acknowledge him. Some people would like to have God as their partner, but they are not willing to have him on his terms. The knowledge we had of the

Scriptures led us to believe that if God were to be our partner, we must at least acknowledge him with a portion of all that with which he blessed us. We realized that we were stewards of all that God let come our way.

3. Both Partners to Be Faithful

Businessmen cannot fail with Christ as their partner. Without him they are already failures. Homes where Jesus has his way do not go on the rocks. Many people never know the joy that comes to the individual, the home, or the business where Christ has been made a partner.

When a young man received God's call to the ministry, it was necessary for him to go away to school. His four hundred acres of beautiful farmland, with the cattle and horses, had to be looked after until all could be sold. A supposedly good friend said to him, "I will see after your farm." The student agreed to let him farm the land one year.

As everything was ready to make the crop, the friend promised to do the work for half the harvest. When time came to sell the cotton, he wrote the student that they should hold the cotton for a better price. This was agreeable. To the student's amazement, when he reached home at Christmastime, the cotton had been sold and all the money had been spent. They were in partnership; they were both to have shared in the increase, but the "friend" took all and gave the student nothing.

Too many people treat God like that. Does God sometimes have to chase us down when we fail to do what he expects of us? Nothing brings more peace and satisfaction to the heart than knowing that God has received us as partners in business with him, and that we have kept our promises to him.

Privileges impose obligations. Citizenship requires taxes. Rights and benefits come with a price tag. "Render therefor unto Caesar the things which are Caesar's; and unto God the things that are God's."

4 Decisions: They Are Yours; Make Them

"Behold, I set before you this day a blessing and a curse; a blessing, if ye obey the commandments of the Lord your God, which I command you this day: and a curse, if ye will not obey the commandments of the Lord your God, but turn aside out of the way which I command you this day, to go after other gods, which ye have not known" (Deut. 11:26–28).

Years ago, a visitor came to America seeking the secret of her greatness. "I went into America's mines, but I did not find the secret to her greatness. I went into her factories, and I did not find it. I went into her legislative halls, and I found it not; but when I heard the preachers of America thundering against sin and unrighteousness—calling America back to God—then I understood the secret to America's greatness." He concluded: "America is great because America is good. When America ceases to be good, America will cease to be great."

One hundred years have passed since that visitor made his tour. Has America ceased to be great? Has she ceased to be good? Is she as good as she was a hundred years ago? America was begun in prayer by people on bended knee, before an open Bible. She was not built on her natural resources, her vast land areas, or her great manpower, although many think so.

The original thirteen colonies were established on religious principles. God blessed this country with all the bounties of heaven. Have we taken these blessings that he has given us and wasted them in riotous living? Many have forgotten God. By some, God has been denied, Christ dethroned, and the Bible defied. Some men deny the divine inspiration of the Scriptures, the virgin birth of Jesus Christ, the efficacy of the atonement, the resurrection of the dead, the judgment, heaven, and hell. A few even contend that God is dead.

Too many schools are taught by unbelievers who deny the tenets of Christian faith. Academic freedom has been interpreted by some preachers as license for revolt and insurrection. Some teachers seek to destroy the system that has built the universities that train them and pay their salaries. What has happened? The Bible holds the answer.

God's message in the book of Malachi is relevant today. "Ye offer polluted bread upon mine altar . . . if ye offer the lame and sick, is it not evil? . . . I have no pleasure in you, saith the Lord of hosts, neither will I accept an offering at your hand. For I am the Lord, I change not; therefore ye sons of Jacob are not consumed" (Mal. 1:7–10; 3:6).

This is God's message to his people in every day and age. The Bible is relevant; it never is out of date. It is both timely and timeless, a message for every age. Christians are God's

Israel of today. Shall we hear what he has to say? Or shall we go the way of every nation that has rejected and forgotten God?

God does not sit idly by and watch with unconcern as his people continue in sin. Sometimes captivity is his way of dealing with his people in bringing them back to his will. This was so in the case of Israel. "Thus saith the Lord, the God of Israel; Like these good figs, so will I acknowledge them that are carried away captive of Judah, whom I have sent out of this place into the land of the Chaldeans for their good" (Jer. 24:5).

Israel was aware of her privilege of choice. God had made plain to his people that their choice would decide their destiny. "Behold, I set before you this day a blessing and a curse; a blessing, if ye obey the commandments of the Lord your God, which I command you this day: and a curse, if ye will not obey the commands of the Lord your God, but turn aside out of the way which I command you this day, to go after other gods, which ye have not known" (Deut. 11:26–28).

Nehemiah had been privileged to bring the children of God out of captivity, back into the homeland. The Temple had been rebuilt. For twelve years this great prophet remained with the people and kept them reminded of the goodness of God and of their responsibilities to him. He took seriously God's word: "For the priest's lips should keep knowledge, and they should seek the law at his mouth: for he is the messenger of the Lord of hosts" (Mal. 2:7).

After twelve years, Nehemiah went back to Persia. The people soon forgot God and drifted back into sin. Then God spoke to his people through his prophet Malachi. God brought his messenger on the scene when the people were steeped in sin. There was a great need for such a prophet in that hour. The people had forsaken God.

A Lesson for Christians Today

The message spoken to Israel through Malachi needs to be considered by Christians today. The United States is a great nation. God has blessed her. She professes to be Christian, yet she continues to drift in the ways of the world.

1. The Spirit Is Willing

At the close of World War I, people realized that God had brought deliverance from the enemy. Liquor and gambling were outlawed. Many sincere people made promises to God. Too soon this privileged nation forgot.

After World War I, a program was launched to share Christ with the nations of the earth. Some leaders seemed to be Christian prophets. Their preaching made a difference. It was thought that with such leadership the world would soon become a spiritual democracy.

2. The Flesh Is Weak

Too soon many forgot. The next quarter of a century, after World War I, the United States drifted back into sin and away from God. Lessons are hard to learn. One generation will not profit by the mistakes of another.

Today the United States has forfeited all right to expect God to continue his blessings. For years God has given this country a place of world leadership, with opportunity to exalt Christ. Instead, she has done that which is right in her own eyes. God's ways have ceased to be our ways.

When the world was in a similar condition, God spoke the message in the book of Malachi.

Shall we profit by this mesage, or will another captivity be necessary?

3. A Warning from God

God has not left his people without warning. He had given Israel instruction that they should remember the sabbath day, to keep it holy; but they had forgotten it. God had warned the people about putting away their wives. God said, "I hate divorce" (Mal. 2:16, RSV). Many in the land had disregarded God's word on this subject and had put their wives away for others. God had told the people of their obligations to him. Yet they had miserably failed. They were satisfied to give God leftovers. Israel robbed God.

God withheld his blessings from his rebellious people. Should he bless us, or are we to anticipate a similar treatment? How do we stand today in regard to the sins charged to Israel? How is our nation on the question of the Lord's Day? How is she on the divorce question? What is our status in honoring God with out substance?

4. A Pitiful Plight

Nations now sleeping in the dust of oblivion began their downfall when they failed to observe God's laws. If these fallen nations could speak, what would they say? God continues to speak. His message to Israel is his message to his people today. If conditions are the same, and since God has not changed nor has his attitude toward sin changed, what can be expected?

When the children of Israel turned from God to sin, God closed the windows of heaven. The people responded with words of complaint. Like many today, they cried out, "Why?"

Israel accused God of not loving her. Therefore, God began his message to Malachi with the words, "I have loved you" (Mal. 1:2). To prove his love and concern for them, God used

43

the illustration of the two nations Israel and Edom, descendants of Jacob and Esau. He showed Israel how the descendants of Esau had suffered ruin and desolation, while those of Jacob had been favored and blessed. Yet they had not responded to his love. Both nations had been captured, but Israel had been released and had returned and rebuilt her Temple and the walls around the city. Yet Edom was still in captivity (Mal. 1:2–5).

God had delivered Israel from captivity, but the people soon forgot. Israel again greatly disappointed God. The people dishonored him. They had not responded to his great love; therefore, he could not bless them in their sins. Some brought leftovers as offerings to God. Finally they said, "It is a tiresome thing to serve him" (Mal. 1:13, author's translation).

As we see the conditions in ancient Israel, let us keep the United States in mind; for the message is also to us. Shall God's warning be heeded?

People Choose God's Blessings or His Curse
1. Sin Dishonors God
Israel belonged to God. He was the Father of that nation. Yet the people failed to honor him. "A son honoureth his father, and a servant his master: if then I be a father [and I am], where is mine honour? And if I be a master [and I am], where is my fear?" (Mal. 1:6).

The nation had not given God the honor a nation should give him, yet they expected his blessings. The United States is treading in Israel's footsteps. Should God bless her? He withheld his blessings from Israel.

Soon after the attack on Pearl Harbor, a little group banded together to push for a swift victory in the war. Pastors were asked to preach one Sunday on the subject "America Will Win the War." The proposed outline for the message had three points: first, we have the material; second, we have the men; third, we will fight. No place was given to the Lord of hosts.

Before me on Sunday morning would sit a mother and two half-sisters of one of the boys who had paid the supreme sacrifice at Pearl Harbor not many days before. They had received a telegram that Connie was at his post of duty on the *Arizona* and was missing in action. What was I to do? Did I have the message for their hearts? Should their pastor bring them a message from God, or should he attempt to console them with anything less? God spoke to their troubled hearts. He was their source of strength and comfort.

God will not be used as an emergency kit in some tight spot. God is on his throne, and men must reckon with him. God will be your partner, but do not leave him out of your plans. The nation or individual that dishonors God will regret it.

If this nation wants God's blessings, then her sons and daughters must get down on their knees and ask his forgiveness. A sin-loving, pleasure-seeking generation must wake up and realize that God must be dealt with. He will not be used, but he desires to use us. He cannot be purchased with leftovers. Others have tried it in the past and have failed.

2. Leftovers Are Not Enough

"Ye offer polluted bread upon the altar" (Mal. 1:7). We do not have to go back to ancient Israel to find people bringing polluted bread and leftovers to God's house.

A church was about to withdraw fellowship

from one of its members. This member never attended worship; in fact, while his pastor preached he sold liquor in an open saloon near the church. Some of the facts had been presented and some discussion had been heard, when the treasurer of the church said: "Brethren, before you take the vote, I wish to say that this man pays about half of the expenses of our church. When you turn him out, you cut the income of the church in half. Every Lord's Day his offering is right here on the table." A hush came over the audience. After a moment, someone arose and said, "Brethren, we had better not turn him out." And they did not.

"And if ye offer the blind for sacrifice, is it not evil? and if ye offer the lame and sick, is it not evil? offer it now unto thy governor; will he be pleased with thee, or accept thy person? saith the Lord of hosts" (Mal. 1:8). God had called for the lamb without spot or blemish, the best of the flock. They had brought that which was of no use to themselves. (See Mal. 1:7–13). God's people had robbed God of that which was his. Could they expect a blessing? Did they deserve a blessing? Polluted bread, leftovers we give to God, and yet we sing "God Bless America." Should God bless America?

Every member of the church should help support the work. Those who cannot should be supported by the church. Often church members say: "We have so many bills, bills, bills—all sorts of bills. By the time we pay the car bill, the gas bill, the light bill, the money is gone. When any money is left, we divide it with God." God will not accept such leftovers.

3. Service to God Should Never Become Tiresome

Israel had grown tired of serving God. Is it

any wonder that God withheld his blessings from them? Their religion had become formal and ritualistic. "Ye said also, Behold, what a weariness is it! and ye have snuffed at it, saith the Lord of hosts; and ye brought that which was torn, and the lame, and the sick; thus ye brought an offering: should I accept this of your hand? saith the Lord. What profit is it that we have kept his ordinance, and that we have walked mournfully before the Lord of hosts?" (Mal. 1:13; 3:14).

The people were tired of serving God, yet they expected his blessings. Many people in America say they are too tired on Sunday to go to church. It is too much to get up and dress for church. Serving God has become tiresome even to many teachers and leaders. It is difficult for many churches to find enough willing people to fill the places of service. People either work too hard through the week or stay out too late Saturday night to be fit for worship on Sunday. What does God think? Should he bless us?

4. Closed Windows Can Be Reopened

Should God bless a country that professes to be Christian, yet often fails to honor him? Should God bless a country that has robbed him as this one has? If even Southern Baptists honored God with their time, talents, service, and substance, perhaps we would know peace. If in the past, when the doors were open to many countries, we had been sending missionaries with God's message rather than robbing God, would these now be Christian nations? But we robbed God. We failed him. Some parents refused to give their sons and daughters as missionaries. Now they are forced to give them, not to go as missionaries but to go with deadly weapons to fight wars. Some Southern Baptists and other

47

Christians refused to respond to the call "Come over into Macedonia, and help us" (Acts 16:9). At times the call is weak, but war clouds continue to overshadow us. More than that, we pay for our folly in blood. Parents pay with sons; wives give up husbands; children lose their fathers.

Years ago when I was pastor of a rural church, a young woman surrendered to foreign mission service. She did not have the education and training for the task, but she was willing to give up her job and work toward that end.

The church observed a "going away" day for her. The hour had come; she was standing at the front of the church as the people marched by and wished her Godspeed. This young woman's mother came down the aisle and put her arms about the daughter and pulled her to the floor. "I had rather see you dead than for you to give your life to some heathen country!" she cried.

The girl's plans were changed. Her mother altered God's plan. She limited the Holy One of Israel. The daughter never went as a missionary.

Should God bless America when she spends more on liquor than on education? Or when she has more saloons than churches? Or when her annual crime bill is billions of dollars?

This is the best time that God's people will ever have to seek his forgiveness and ask him to teach us to appreciate his blessings. It is mockery for us to act as we do and then sing "God Bless America." One cannot expect more from unregenerate people, but more is expected from blood-bought, sin-forgiven children of God. When God's people get right with God, there will not be standing room in the churches. Budgets will be enlarged; God's storehouse will overflow; missionaries will go everywhere there is need with God's message of redemption.

48

5 The Bible and Your Responsibility

*"Study to shew thyself approved unto God, a
workman that needeth not to be ashamed,
rightly dividing the word of truth" (2 Tim. 2:15).*

The average life of the world's
great civilizations has been about two hundred
years. Our country is at this milestone. Shall
we go the way of other nations? Or will we
return to God and be used by him?

Christians seeking freedom from bondage
came to this country and in sacrifice and blood
left us a great heritage. Faith gave them courage
even to die for liberty. Many times bondage is
God's only way to bring his people back from
sin. If the United States is to be saved, Christian
people must do it. If God is depending upon
Southern Baptists to have a part in preaching
the gospel to all nations, then it is time to act.

49

Statisticians estimate that one person out of twenty that ever lived lives today. What a challenge! People! All kinds of people! Multitudes with outstretched arms beckon to us.

A pagan world is moving in on us. The population of the world is increasing thirty times faster than the number of people touched by all Christian missionaries. For years Southern Baptists reached more people than the next six largest denominations together reached. God had given Baptists the know-how. He blessed our efforts. People were reached. Every phase of church life increased in proportion to the number of people reached for Bible study.

For years the pastors baptizing the most people testified that 90 percent of their baptisms came through the Sunday School. True evangelism acknowledges the vital role of a Sunday School in reaching people for Christ. It is the right arm of a church in quest for souls and a must in perennial evangelism.

God took Ezekiel out to show him a city that was a graveyard. He gave Ezekiel the remedy: talk to these dead people in behalf of God, and talk to God in behalf of them. God's plan has not changed. The best way to change a graveyard into a live New Testament church is to enlist those dead in sin in Bible study, teach them the Word of God, then pray for the Holy Spirit to do his work.

James L. Sullivan, president of the Sunday School Board of the Southern Baptist Convention, said: "The results of the 'A Million More in '54' campaign should teach us the relationship between enlistment of people and the resultant growth of a denomination. Church and denominational growth among Southern Baptists realized their most rapid strides as the Sunday

School was making its most progressive steps forward. Baptisms, church membership, numbers of churches established, and so on, came rapidly on the heels of the Sunday School advance. This is always true. No organization or movement will go beyond the Bible teaching, people-reaching unit of the local churches, the Sunday School.

"People must be reached, else everything bogs. The Sunday School is to be the spearhead of advance and without progress at this point all else suffers correspondingly. Even Church Training knew its greatest period of growth when the Sunday School was moving forward the fastest through the 'A Million More in '54' campaign. This experience holds in the whole church life."

The pastor is responsible for the success or failure of a church to reach people. If a New Testament church is to stay forever after people, the pastor must lead. The day a New Testament church ceases to reach people, it begins to die.

By "reaching people," I do not mean simply winning people to Christ, as important as that is. Salvation from sin is not enough. God saves from sin, but he saves for something else. Evangelism is not complete until the evangelized become evangelists. "And his gifts were that some should be apostles, some prophets, some evangelists, some pastors and teachers, for the equipment of the saints, for the work of the ministry, for building up the body of Christ until we all attain to the unity of the faith and of the knowledge of the Son of God, to mature manhood, to the measure of the stature of the fulness of Christ" (Eph. 4:11–13, RSV). This is what "reaching people" means. It is not enough to win them to Christ; we must follow

51

through. Reaching people involves beginning with each person where he is, lost and ruined because of sin, and following through until he comes "to the measure of the stature of the fulness of Christ" (Eph. 4:13, RSV).

Salvation of a soul takes place in regeneration. Salvation of a life is a continual process. Reaching people is done only as the one located and enlisted in Bible study is won to Christ and is doing "all things whatsoever I have commanded you" (Matt. 28:20). What a challenge!

The Word and the Spiritually Dead

"Can these bones live?" God asked Ezekiel. The situation seemed hopeless to the preacher, but he obeyed God. A graveyard is a place for the dead. All people apart from him who said, "I am the life" are dead.

God's picture of a city of lost people is a graveyard. Yet such people do not know they are dead until they are told. This requires both human and divine effort. In response to God's question, Ezekiel said, "Thou knowest." Then God revealed to him his method of causing the spiritually dead to live. The Christian's part is to witness to the dead, then pray that the Holy Spirit will give life to the dead. Jesus said, "The time now is when the dead shall hear the voice of God and live" (John 5:25, author's paraphrase).

1. To Be Educated Is Not Enough

The caption in a magazine read, "Celestial engineers, heavy thinkers, analyzing the future." When these statements caught my eye, I thought, Surely this article is about Bible preachers and teachers. To my amazement, I found that the "celestial engineers" were not Bible preachers and teachers at all. They were employees of a business concern in the scientific world. These men were educated, but that does not mean they were not lost. Being educated does not give men eternal life.

We are amazed by man's progress in the scientific world. Man has learned to use God's creation for his purposes. But too few know the Savior who gives them life. Front-page headlines disclosed the unveiling of a hypersonic airplane that cruises at seven thousand miles an hour, forty miles high. Master minds conceived and engineered this machine. These are educated men. Some are educated but lost.

Educated people are everywhere. Many are scientifically alert, yet spiritually dead. Some have never been reached for Jesus Christ. Education is needful, but it is not enough. Lost men need the Savior.

2. To Be Religious Is Not Enough

The Pharisees were most religious, yet Jesus called them hypocrites, "whited sepulchres." Paul saw that the people of Athens were very religious, yet they knew not the God whom Paul preached as the Savior of the world.

To be religious is not enough. All the religions of the world will not save one lost sinner. Many religious people are lost. Only Christ can save. Jesus said, " 'Unless you believe that I am He, you shall die in your sins' " (John 8:24, NASB).[1]

There are more religious sects in the United States today than there are in all other parts of the world. Most countries have several religions; America has too many "isms" to count. Were the apostle Paul to visit the United States and see the numerous sects, he would have reason

··········
[1] From the *New American Standard Bible.* © The Lockman Foundation, La Habra, California, 1971. Published by Creation House, Carol Stream, Illinois.

to preach to the people "the unknown God." Bones, dry bones, are everywhere. What are we doing about it? Are churches reaching people?

3. Only the Living Lord Can Raise the Dead

Ezekiel's congregation was a pathetic sight. Dry bones were scattered everywhere: dead, lifeless bones, bones bleached by the tropical sun. God commanded Ezekiel, "Prophesy to these bones in behalf of God and prophesy to God in behalf of these bones." When Ezekiel spoke in behalf of God, there was a rattling of bones. Bone came to bone. When the bones had properly assembled, God put flesh, sinews, and skin upon them. Still there was no life. God said to Ezekiel, "Now, speak to God in behalf of these bones." When Ezekiel followed God's command, God breathed life into the dead bodies. They lived. (See Ezek. 37:1–14.)

This could take place daily in every community if God's will were done. The spiritually dead are everywhere. People are dead in trespasses and sin. The only hope for them is for Jesus Christ to come into their hearts. The method Jesus uses is for someone to speak to these people in behalf of God.

Sunday School teachers are adequate to get the message of salvation, the Word of God, to these people. They have the know-how. They know how to locate people. Sunday School workers have learned how to enlist unreached people for Bible study. Teachers are trained to teach the Word of God. When Bible teachers have spoken to the people on behalf of God and then to God on behalf of the people, God will give his blessing.

Teachers may locate, enlist, teach, and pray; but God gives the increase. The new birth is the work of the Holy Spirit. A Bible teacher has a glorious task. Churches that train from 15 to

20 percent of the membership as teachers of the Word make it possible for more of these bones to live.

The Power of the Word of God
1. Preaching the Word

A few years ago most of us thought it impossible to go to the moon. Now men have walked on the moon and even in outer space. This has been accomplished at great risk and expense. Nothing has been allowed to hinder this moon exploration. Now that we have explored the moon, our attention is being turned to other planets.

The Bible does not reveal whether God wanted man to land on the moon, but it does tell us that he is depending upon his people to preach the gospel to every creature on earth. God expects Southern Baptists to give the gospel of Christ to all nations. The business of every New Testament church is to "preach the gospel to every creature" (Mark 16:15) and to disciple the nations.

As the scientific world has been moon conscious, Christians must be conscious of a lost world and their responsibility to get the redemptive message of Christ to all people. The business of every Christian is set forth in the Bible in such simple language that there is no reason for misunderstanding. The task of a church is clearly outlined. "And he said unto them, Go ye into all the world, and preach the gospel to every creature" (Mark 16:15). Could Jesus have made it plainer?

The pulpit regulates the climate in a church. Southern Baptist churches will keep the pulpit in the center of the church. They believe the Holy Spirit spoke through the apostle Paul when he said, "It pleased God by the foolishness of preaching to save them that believe" (1 Cor. 1:21). There is power in the preached Word of God. "The preaching of the cross is to them that perish foolishness; but to us which are saved it is the power of God" (1 Cor. 1:18). If the battle is lost in a church, it is lost in the pulpit. Any activity of a church not worthy of support from the pulpit should not be in the church calendar.

Jesus came preaching. People pressed upon him to hear the Word of God. Jesus expects his followers to preach. "Let the dead bury their dead: but go thou and preach" (Luke 9:60).

There is nothing more important than preaching. A New Testament church is responsible for preaching. God still makes this possible by calling preachers. Southern Baptists have more than nine thousand preachers in their schools preparing for a lifetime ministry of preaching.

Several years ago, Southern Baptists of California were in a campaign to start one hundred churches in one day. The machinery was rolling; churches were responding; pastors were happy. In one of the meetings a man asked, "If we start one hundred churches, where in the world will we get the preachers?"

That was an easy question. I replied: "It is our business to start the churches. God calls preachers."

In one church that started seven missions in twenty-six months, God called from the congregation a preacher for each mission. After the sixth mission was started, God called a seventh preacher. One of the deacons said to his pastor, "Either we miscalculated or God made a mistake in calling an extra preacher." The church started another mission.

The Word of God is essential in preaching. It

is the only message to preach for the spiritual resurrection of the spiritually dead.

2. Teaching the Word

No great movement comes to fruition without teaching. The most important of all movements was started by Jesus. He placed so much stress upon teaching that a ruler of the Jews said to him, "Rabbi [Master], we know that thou art a teacher come from God" (John 3:2). Projects involving people cannot succeed without teaching. Teaching requires teachers. "Teaching them to observe all things whatsoever I have commanded you" (Matt. 28:20) was no play on words by Jesus. This is a distinct part of his commission to his church.

Paul reminded young Timothy of the need to be "apt to teach . . . in meekness instructing those . . ." (2 Tim. 2:24–25). Paul realized, as every preacher must, that "I am appointed a preacher . . . and a teacher" (2 Tim. 1:11).

For forty years Southern Baptists enlarged their teaching ministry through their Sunday Schools. Year by year they continued to grow. They followed a few simple but fundamental principles of growth in reaching the multitudes for Bible study. These basic laws of growth have not changed. Churches that obey these laws continue to reach more people for Bible study. Bible teaching that uses the saved in prophesying to the dead involves finding the dead. Christians must not overlook the graveyard nearest home. God expects the scope of the work of every Christian to include not only Jerusalem but " 'Judea and Samaria and to the end of the earth' " (Acts 1:8, RSV).

Teaching the Word involves enlisting and training teachers. God has enough potential teachers if they are sought out, enlisted, and trained to do his work. These will survey the graveyards, prophesy to the bones, and pray for the Holy Spirit to do what only he can do—raise the dead. The pastor who knows how to build and maintain an organization can keep his church growing with a constant stream of new people. In fact, the pastor who learns this secret can decide "how many." He can reach as many people as he plans to reach. Churches with less than 20 percent of the membership teaching the Bible every Sunday are not reaching the people they could reach.

Recently a member of another large denomination said to a Southern Baptist: "There is nothing known to man that compares to your Sunday School program of reaching people." Leaders from many major denominations have gone to Ridgecrest and Glorieta to learn our program and methods.

Other denominational groups are reaching people with tested, successful methods that for years Southern Baptists used to reach people in large numbers. A worker in a Baptist Book Store said, "It is amazing how others continue to use the methods books that Southern Baptists once used."

Have Southern Baptists lost concern for people? Why are many churches reaching fewer people year by year?

Too many Southern Baptist churches are looking for an easy way to reach people. They have not found it. Outreach has been shortened. The number of unreached people is alarming. Yet many refuse to practice what they know has been successful in the past.

Growing churches come out of growing Sunday Schools, not growing Sunday Schools out of growing churches. Enrollment and attendance increase in direct proportion to ten pupils for one teacher or unit. To start new teaching units is to reach more people.

Departments and classes reach their maximum growth in about a year. Common sense then should teach the need to start more units and put more people to work. Grading by age is one practical way to set up new units. Growth demands a larger pattern, and space holds the key.

New units reach people faster, and the fastest growing churches are constantly starting new units. We have learned by experience that to combine two classes means they soon become the size of one. But put two teachers to work and the number of people reached is doubled. Another rule is that when average attendance drops, enrollment is too large per teaching unit. When average attendance in Sunday School declines, start another class.

Recently a successful pastor said, "The difference in churches is leadership, and the difference in leaders is training." Any church can and should have all the workers it needs. There never has been more stress on specialization than in our day. People have learned the necessity of specialized training. The business world has taught us this, yet many churches have not learned the lesson. Jesus said, "The children of this world are in their generation wiser than the children of light" (Luke 16:8). Teachers must be trained to meet growing skills and needs. The pastor more than anyone else is responsible for training Christian teachers to reach and teach every available prospect.

3. Witnessing with the Word

When Andrew found the Lord, he did not wait for a study course on soul-winning. He did not have anyone to explain to him how hard it would be to find his brother and bring him to Jesus. But he had an experience worth telling. He had a witness to bear. With words that thrilled and burned, Andrew told his brother what Jesus had done for him. "And he brought him to Jesus" (John 1:42). Perhaps he did not know about stewardship, but he felt a responsibility.

Witnessing has been made so complex in recent years that Christians are afraid to try it. Pastors spend hours preaching about soul-winning, but little time is spent in doing it. Study course after study course is taught on witnessing. Teachers have frightened the average Christian. They have made witnessing so difficult that it seems to require a professional. It has lost its challenge to the average Christian.

A personal testimony has much power. Christians should be urged to give their testimony in an effort to introduce others to Jesus. A witness knows something; he has something to tell. To tell it at the right time to the right person as the Holy Spirit leads is all the Lord requires. With this men can be, and are, brought to Jesus.

Power for Witnessing Comes from the Holy Spirit

1. Promised for This Purpose

In a revival service the evangelist said: "There are two activities in my experience when I can feel beyond any doubt the power of the Holy Spirit present and at work. One is when I am preaching Jesus, and the other is when I am witnessing to a lost person." For this, the Christian can be assured of the power of the Holy Spirit.

Power is promised and available for witnessing. When Jesus said to his followers, "Make disciples," he assured them of the power of the Holy

Spirit. Then he said, "And ye shall be witnesses unto me" (Acts 1:8).

Moments before Jesus ascended to the right hand of the Father, he said to his disciples, "Go ye into all the world, and preach the gospel to every creature" (Mark 16:15). Suddenly he was gone. The disciples "went forth, and preached every where, the Lord working with them, and confirming the word with signs following" (Mark 16:20).

How could it be made more simple? Who could misunderstand this? Jesus never intended for his followers to be inadequate for the task he assigned them. He made power available for the task. This power is promised for preaching and teaching the gospel. Power is withheld until workers get to the main task.

This power cannot be bought, or some would purchase it. People have sought to buy it. Simon Peter said, "Thy money perish with thee, because thou hast thought that the gift of God may be purchased with money" (Acts 8:20).

The way to this power is clear. Jesus is the same yesterday, today, and forever. He has not changed, nor has his promise been broken.

What is happening in churches today? Business as usual? There is no confirmation of the Word with signs following? Why? Could it be that we work without the Lord working with us? Power is available to those who meet his conditions.

2. Demonstrated for Our Example

When the Holy Spirit does not have complete control of a person, there is no power. One day a troubled father brought his demon-possessed son to the disciples for help. They tried but they could not help him. They stood powerless. Plans are essential, organization is necessary, and programs are good; but unless the Holy Spirit's power produces signs, there will be none. Without the Spirit, Christians are helpless. Many of us follow orders, run the machinery, observe the rules, say the word, yet demons come not out.

Those willing to do the Spirit's bidding may know his power. Those surrendering to his will may expect that witnessing will result. Philip is a good example. "Then the Spirit said unto Philip, Go near, and join thyself to this chariot. And Philip ran thither to him . . . . Then Philip opened his mouth, and began at the same scripture, and preached unto him Jesus". (Acts 8:29–35). Immediately the man trusted Jesus and was saved.

When the Holy Spirit controls, one's influence will count for Christ. This was true of Paul. "And after he had seen the vision, immediately we endeavored to go into Macedonia, assuredly gathering that the Lord had called us for to preach the gospel unto them" (Acts 16:10). Lydia and many others accepted Christ as their Lord and Savior.

Christ will be honored and glorified in and through a Holy Spirit-filled life. "He shall glorify me: for he shall receive of mine, and shall shew it unto you" (John 16:14). When God's will is done, there will be power for the task. Power is promised for witnessing. Jesus said, "All power is given unto me in heaven and in earth" (Matt. 28:18). He also said, "Tarry ye in the city of Jerusalem, until ye be endued with power from on high" (Luke 24:49).

The world is the field; making disciples is the task. Southern Baptists know how to reach people. Their organizations are superb, and they are essential. Yet the Holy Spirit must give direction and power for success. Only Spirit-filled lives have power. "Then he answered and spake unto me, saying, This is the word of the Lord unto Zerubbabel, saying, not by might, nor by power, but by my spirit, saith the Lord of hosts" (Zech. 4:6).

6 Your Brother Is Your Responsibility; Win Him

"And the Lord said unto Cain, Where is Abel thy brother? And he said, I know not; Am I my brother's keeper?" (Gen. 4:9).

Both the Old and New Testaments describe the attitude and works of Cain as evil, but the conduct of Abel his brother is called righteous. Each brother brought an offering to God. The offering of Cain was a display of his ability. In no way did his offering indicate his unworthy and sinful attitude and life. There was nothing in what he brought to acknowledge his weakness and his dependence upon God. His spirit and his offering gave no evidence of a sense of sin.

Abel's offering was a blood offering. Feeling his guilt and in recognition of his sin, Abel displayed a broken and a contrite heart. His attitude was one of humility and confession. The Bible tells us that God rejected the offering of Cain and that he was well pleased with that of Abel.

In the sight of God there is a vast difference in a display of our efforts and an offering for our sins. God's rejection of Cain's offering sent him into a jealous rage which he took out on his innocent brother Abel. At the first opportunity, Cain killed his brother.

When he heard the cry of Abel's innocent blood, God confronted the slayer with the question, "Where is Abel thy brother?" (Gen. 4:9). It is impossible to deal with the stewardship of life without answering this question.

Too many stewards respond to this age-old question with one answer, "Am I my brother's keeper?" Until one is ready to answer correctly this question, "Am I my brother's keeper?" he is not responding to the will of God.

Every Christian must face this question. The response each gives will determine whether he is a good or bad steward.

This question is at the heart of stewardship. Jesus summed up the commandments, "Thou shalt love the Lord thy God with all thy heart, and with all thy soul, and with all thy strength, and with all thy mind; and thy neighbour as thyself" (Luke 10:27). What is left? What is Christian stewardship but one's duty to God and to man? If one is to be rightly related to God on the one hand and to his neighbor on the other, he must have divine help.

Do You Know Your Brother?

Many professed Christians have problems at this point. Willingness to accept every man as he is and to recognize him as one's responsibility is the God-given duty of every Christian. In order to accept one's responsibility for his brother, one must know where he is.

Cain knew where his brother was. He was responsible for his condition. God faced Cain with his responsibility. We do not have to slay our brother to bring dishonor to God and disgrace to ourselves. We need only neglect him.

It was not easy for God to get Ezekiel to locate his brother. This prophet was taken to the valley of dry bones where he could know who, where, and in what condition the people were. It was not until he saw the scattered bones that Ezekiel felt his responsibility for the helpless people who had no knowledge of God and his will for their lives.

Human nature has not changed across the centuries. It is still difficult today for God to get his servants to find out who and where their lost brothers are.

Paul Paid His Debt to His Brothers

The Bible reveals in Paul a good steward. To the elders of Ephesus he said, "I testify to you this day that I am innocent of the blood of all of you" (Acts 20:26, RSV). Paul wanted it recorded that he had discharged his whole duty to the people for whom he was responsible.

How many of us can make this claim for ourselves? Until we as stewards can say this, we have not fulfilled our duty to God or our responsibility to the unsaved. I do have an obligation to my brother. To neglect or refuse this responsibility is to rebel against the God who gave his Son to die for my sins. I must accept this stewardship responsibility.

To say with Paul, "I am guilty of no man's blood," suggests the kind of stewardship God expects of us. When we do what Paul did, we can say what he said. He said, "I have not shunned to declare unto you the whole counsel of God" (Acts 20:27). Before we can wash our hands of the blood of our lost brothers, we must declare unto them the claims of Jesus Christ upon their lives.

Herein lies the great burden for souls upon those who are saved. Every person within my responsibility must hear the Word. I must see to this. Paul was a faithful steward. God expects no less from you and me.

What will it take for the Lord to thrust us out into the highways, dirt roads, apartments, and suburbs? This he has commanded of us, yet few have given even partial consideration to his command.

This text is a call to arms. Christian soldiers, it is time for us to face up to our duty to God and to our fellowman. We need to gird up the loins of our faith, put on the breastplate of righteousness, and get at it. This is our responsibility.

A pastor gave to a Sunday School teacher the name of an unsaved boy. He asked that she witness to him. She did repeatedly, but with no favorable response. She accepted her responsibility well. She worked hard. She did her best, but that rebellious boy broke her heart.

Later the boy suffered a fatal illness. This faithful teacher went to her pastor in tears, but with a conviction that she had done her best. She had discharged her responsibility to an unsaved boy.

This is what this Scripture passage is about. This is my task and yours. When you meet Jesus, can you say with this Christian teacher, "I did my best"? Our best is all that God requires. But we cannot do less than our best.

Christians Have a Duty to Warn Non-Christians

God said to Ezekiel, "Warn them for me" (Ezek. 33:7). He expects no less of you and me. Paul said: "Christ in you, the hope of glory: whom we preach, warning every man, and teaching every man in all wisdom; that we may present every man [who will] perfect in Christ Jesus" (Col. 1:27–28).

Our Lord commanded, "As ye go, make disciples." This is your job and mine. It is every Christian's job. The call to duty is, "As my Father hath sent me, even so send I you" (John 20:21). Jesus spoke these words. Will we heed what he said?

This Is God's Method

Perhaps you have wondered, Why did not God send a legion of angels to earth and witness to every unsaved person and finish the task? Why obligate human beings with this giant task when angels could have done it so easily?

When Cornelius was seeking to know the will of God, God sent an angel to his home. But the angel was not sent to tell him how to be saved. God had said that those who seek him shall find him, but angels are for other purposes than to reveal salvation.

While Cornelius prayed and offered up alms to God, an angel came to tell him where he could find a sinner saved by grace who could give true witness to this salvation. The angel was not to explain the plan of salvation to Cornelius, for he had never had this experience. Simon Peter was resting on top of a house, across country at Joppa. The angel told Cornelius to send for Simon Peter, who could come and bear witness to his need. Peter had been saved and could explain his experience of salvation.

Only those who have had salvation's experience can bear true witness to this grace. Read Acts 10:6 and 11:14. The angel left without telling Cornelius how to be redeemed. God does not commission angels to witness, for they have not been redeemed. He commissions saved sinners. They have had the experience, and the redeemed are to say so. Witnessing is the privilege and obligation of every Christian.

When Saul of Tarsus was stricken down on the way to Damascus, his instructions were to go to one who was a believer in Christ. Ananias was to witness to Paul, though Christ himself confronted him. When Saul said, "Lord what wilt thou have me to do?" (Acts 9:6), Jesus told him that Ananias, one who had been redeemed, would explain the plan of salvation to him.

God is not depending on angels to testify to his saving grace. He is depending on you and me. Will it be that many for whom you are responsible will die in their sins because you failed to warn them? Personal witnessing is God's method.

A group of men were arguing one day in front of a post office over whether the heathen would be saved without the gospel. The postmaster went into his office, brought out his Bible, and read from Romans: "For whosoever shall call upon the name of the Lord shall be saved. How then shall they call on him in whom they have not believed? and how shall they believe in him of whom they have not heard? and how shall they hear without a preacher?" (Rom. 10:13–14). The postmaster walked back to his desk, deposited his Bible, and the men began talking about something else.

Am I my brother's keeper? Am I concerned enough to find him? Do I know who he is, or am I concerned enough to find out?

The Bible says, "He that winneth souls is wise" (Prov. 11:30) "and they that be wise shall shine as the brightness of the firmament; and they that turn many to righteousness [shall shine] as the stars for ever and ever" (Dan. 3:3).

There is no better way to find my brother, to know who he is and where he is, than to go from house to house taking a religious census of the community. For some time our church has surveyed a section of our community each quarter. This has proved to be an effective way to find prospects. More than that, this reveals to our community the genuine concern of our church for the people of the area.

None of us wants to meet Jesus in judgment with blood on our hands. Let us discharge our stewardship as faithful witnesses.

Early one morning a faithful member of our church called and said, "Pastor, don't give me away, but I feel that my next-door neighbors would decide for Jesus today if you could drop in." Before eight-thirty I knocked on the door of the neighbor. He must have been nearby, for the door opened before I had ceased knocking. I said: "Good morning; I am Charles McKay, the pastor of First Southern Baptist Church."

So astonished was the man that instead of asking me in he turned around and called out: "Wife! Come! Here is a preacher now." Then this preacher received a warm and gracious invitation from the two to come in.

It was easy to know immediately that the woman who had called me knew what she was doing. The man opened the discussion with all

70

sincerity of his soul because he was then under conviction. My faithful church member had been witnessing to this couple both from her experience and the Bible. The man said: "Preacher, we have not slept all night. For the first time in our lives we realize that we are lost and we need to be saved. Can you help us?"

I opened my New Testament and read to the man the claims of Jesus Christ upon his life. Then I asked him if he would join me on his knees to ask God to forgive him and save him. I prayed first, thanking God for the conviction for sin that I sensed in the man. Then, as simply as a child, I asked God to save the man and let him know it the second he believed. Before closing the prayer, I thanked God for saving him. By that time this man began calling upon God to forgive him and save him.

Before getting off our knees, I asked my new friend if by putting his hand into mine he would say, "I am trusting Jesus as my Lord and Savior." His hand clasped mine as he said, "Yes." The moment he did this, God saved him. He crawled on his knees around in front of his beautiful wife, grabbed her around the waist, and said: "Honey, I'm saved! Don't you want to be too?"

With words that thrilled and burned, he gave to his wife his testimony, and she too was gloriously saved. This is the Christian's God-given responsibility to his brother.

7 Your Influence: Guard It

"For none of us liveth to himself, and no man dieth to himself" (Rom 14:7).
"Moreover it is required in stewards, that a man be found faithful" (1 Cor. 4:2).
"Let your light so shine before men, that they may see your good works, and glorify your Father which is in heaven" (Matt. 5:16).

Late in life a man heard the gospel and accepted Jesus Christ as his Lord and Savior. He had no idea that evening when he went to the revival that such an experience would be his. His conversion made such a difference in him that he did not immediately return home.

This saved drunkard decided that he must make amends to those he had wronged during his wicked life. First he stopped at a home to pay a man a debt that for years he had refused to pay. He called several people from their beds to apologize for his unchristian conduct and abuse of them before he was saved. But his hardest task that night was to go to the ceme-tery. There he wept over the grave where lay the body of his son who had died drunk. The newly saved father looked to heaven and cried, "Oh, God, here is one wrong I can't undo."

Generals have won battles by proxy. Men have amassed fortunes by proxy. Kings have ruled by proxy. But people must die personally. "It is appointed unto men once to die" (Heb. 9:27). Man dies, but his influence never dies.

No Man Lives unto Himself

Some people live as if they were not account-able to others and ultimately to God for the way they live. Every human being is responsible both to God and to his fellowman. Just as every tree casts its shadow, so every man has influ-ence. Good or bad, our deeds follows us.

A mother was talking with her teenage daughter about what had happened in a rap session of young people with their counselor. The counselor had called for testimonies from young people who wished to name a person who had been a good influence on them. When the name of one person was called, someone asked, "Is that man like that all the time, or does he just act like that around us?" The teenager said: "Mother, I told them that this man is my grand-father, that I have known him almost eighteen years, and that he is always the same. He is the same at home and everywhere else."

Influence Is a Stewardship Trust

1. Man Is Responsible for His Influence

It is inspiring to read from the Bible words such as, "He did that which was right in the sight of the Lord" (2 Chron. 29:2). These men of God had their weaknesses as well as we. But they were single-hearted. They were not double-minded. The thrust of their lives glorified God. Their chief concern was to follow God's will. The influence of such men calls us to a deeper stewardship of life.

David Livingstone became so obsessed with God's will for him that he planted his life in Africa. One night, after a siege of sickness, he was found on his knees as if in prayer but dead. The Africans buried his heart in his beloved Africa. England buried his body in Westminster Abbey as a hero. John Knox was so dedicated to the will of God and his influence was so powerful for the influence of Christ that he was feared by Scotland.

During seminary days, a friend of mine was called home to the funeral of a relative. In his funeral message the preacher stressed the power and responsibility of influence. A good man, but an unprofessed Christian, came forward during the funeral and asked the people to forgive him for the wrong influence he had had on others by staying out of church. He confessed that for years he had been a believer in Jesus Christ and was sure of his salvation but had never made a public profession of faith. He asked the people to receive him that day into the church fellowship. They did.

When my friend returned to the seminary campus, he told me that twenty-five adults followed this man down the aisle at the funeral, making public their decision to follow Christ. Most of the twenty-five acknowledged that this good man, while an unprofessed Christian, almost caused them to go to hell. They said that he was the best man they knew.

I had rather my children and my grandchildren one day stand over my grave and say,

"My daddy (or my granddaddy) was the best Christian man I knew" than to leave them millions of dollars.

2. Harmful Influence Is Unfair to Others

Some good men allow their influence to be hurtful to others. Jotham, king of Israel, was a good man. "And he did that which was right in the sight of the Lord, according to all that his father Uzziah did: howbeit he entered not into the temple of the Lord. And the people did yet corruptly" (2 Chron. 27:2). Most of the kings of Israel could not have this said of them. "They did evil in the sight of the Lord" is written concerning many of them. Jotham was one of the few of whom it was said that he was a good man. We are not surprised, however, when we read that his father Uzziah, who reigned fifty-two years, "did that which was right in the sight of the Lord" (2 Chron. 26:4). And we can understand even better as we read that his grandfather Amaziah "did that which was right in the sight of the Lord" (2 Chron. 25:2).

Jotham had a good background. The influence of his father and his grandfather was good. There is no way to measure the worth of godly parents and grandparents. Jotham was king by birth, but he was more than that. He was a good man. His leadership qualities made him equal to his task.

Jotham was a hard worker. No one ever accused him of being lazy. He built cities, castles, towers, and the high gate to the Temple. "Jotham became mighty, because he prepared his ways before the Lord his God" (2 Chron. 27:6).

Only one evil influence is mentioned in the Bible against this good man: he did not attend the worship at the Temple. The Bible does not tell us why this good man did not attend the house of God. Perhaps he had this feelings hurt.

Many for trivial reasons have joined those who forsake the assembling of themselves together at God's house. If the harm stopped here, it might be less serious; but we cannot leave evil influence here. The same verse that says Jotham was a good man, continues: "Howbeit he entered not into the temple of the Lord. And the people did yet corruptly" (2 Chron. 27:2).

The Tragedy of Bad Influence

A man may be morally upright. He may be a loving father and husband. He does not have to be a cheat or covetous to wield the wrong influence. A person can be a good provider for his family and have the wrong influence on them. It is easy for a good person to cancel all the good he does with one or two unwise acts.

By his failure to attend the Temple worship, Jotham erased not only his good influence but that of his father and grandfather as well. "The people did . . . corruptly" tells the story. The good influences of Amaziah, the grandfather, caused the people to do right in the sight of God. The same was true of the good influence of Jotham's father Uzziah. But the people who were influenced by Jotham did not follow his good traits. They let his one weakness turn them from doing right in the sight of God.

Some people today are like Jotham. They are not against the church. They would not want to live in a community without a church. Some give to the church to prove their interest. Yet they forsake the assembling of themselves together. Some parents have returned to the church after leading their children off into a far country of sin, but their children will not return. This breaks a father's or a mother's heart. Some

parents wait too late to return to the fellowship
of the church.

The evil influence of Jotham was enough to
cause his father and his grandfather to turn
over in their graves. Ahaz, the son of Jotham,
came to the throne, and the Word of God records,
"He [Ahaz] did not that which was right in the
sight of the Lord" (2 Chron. 28:1). He built
altars and images to Baalim (28:2). Ahaz "burnt
his children in the fire, after the abominations of
the heathen" (28:3). He shut the door to the
house of God (2 Chron. 28:24).

To every person God offers life or death, blessings or cursings. Each decides which it will be.
Eventually the day of reckoning is coming. What
we have and are belongs to God. We must give
account to him. His word to us is, "Occupy till
I come." Influence will be active until the Judge
returns.

George W. Truett was one of my favorite
preachers. He had a strong influence upon my
life, even though I heard him preach only a few
times. This princely preacher had closed his
message. The service was concluded, and the
pastor stood at the door speaking to his congregation. After everyone had left the auditorium,
Dr. Truett went to get his Bible. He was surprised to find a sobbing man still sitting in a
pew. The preacher went over to offer his help.
The man began to explain his grief. Dr. Truett's
text had struck this man with conviction: "None
of us liveth to himself, and no man dieth to
himself" (Rom. 14:7). "Pastor, you remember
that I was sixty-eight years old when I was
saved," the man explained. "This morning I
came by the home of my son and urged him to
come with me to church. He refused. He said:
'Dad, I've plenty of time to give attention to

religion. I'm not near sixty-eight.' Preacher, I started on my way to church with a broken heart. When I passed by my grandchildren playing in the yard, I asked them if they wouldn't go with me to church. Glancing at one another and then at me, they said: 'Granddad, you remember how old you were when you started going to church. We have a long time yet. We'll go someday.' "

"Oh, Pastor," he said, "I would have my arm cut off if I could undo my influence, if I could go back and live before my children and grandchildren as a man ought to live."

A man may die, but his influence lives on.

8 Your Talents: You Can Multiply Them

"To every man according to his several ability" (*Matt. 25:15*).

The English word "stewardship" comes from two words, sty and weard, meaning a pig-pen guard. This means one who is in charge of the property of another. Jesus said, "Take away from him who uses not and give to one who will." There was a reason for taking away the little that one has to give to another.

All men are created equal. God is no respecter of persons; he gives every man a chance to prove himself faithful. This does not mean that God gives all men the same native gift or ability. Not all men are given equal advantages. Therefore, all men are not held accountable for the same achievement. Each man is given opportunity to be faithful where he is with what he has.

All Men Are Not Given the Same Abilities

"Unto one [servant] he gave five talents, to another two, and to another one" (Matt. 25:15). On one side of a talent is written "endowment" and on the other "responsibility." Every person is held accountable to the measure of his ability. To exchange talents with one's neighbor would be to exchange obligations also with him. God measures responsibility by opportunity.

Our Talents Are Not Our Own

In the parable of the talents (Matt. 25:14–30), when the owner went away, he assigned his talents to his servants. He left five talents with one, two with another, and one with a third. The servants were instructed to use the talents while their master was away. They were to give an account upon his return. These abilities were not properties of these servants; they belonged to their master.

Our talents are not our own. They belong to God, and they must be used for his glory. Paul asked, "What hast thou that thou didst not receive?" (1 Cor. 4:7). He also said, "We brought nothing into this world, and it is certain we can carry nothing out" (1 Tim. 6:7). In 1 Corinthians 12, Paul said that there are diversities of gifts, but the same Spirit gives them. God gives as he wills, his own talents to his own creation. It is not ours to question how many or for what, but it is ours to use what he gives us.

Those talents you have—where did you get them? God is the owner; they belong to him. We owe to God a responsibility to use our talents for his glory. We are to watch after and use our talents as the guard watches over his master's pigs in the pen. Every steward should live daily as though at the end of the day, or even before, he would be called in to give account of his stewardship to the owner.

Christ gives gifts unto men, but they are still his. He gives them according to his own pleasure. So then, our talents are not ours but his. They are on consignment to us.

We Must Use God's Talents for His Glory

We are stewards of God's talents, and we should be good stewards. Every man is a steward, good or bad. Which are you?

God's talents should be used for his work. Some use God's talents for the devil's work. "To every man his work" (see Mark 13:34). No one can do your work. Only you have the ability for it, so do it.

Paul said, "That I may lay hold on that for which also I was laid hold on by Christ Jesus" (Phil. 3:12, ASV). God has a work for everyone. He is counting on us. He has given us the talents with which to work. We must not fail him. Paul was ever pressing on, trying to do what God had assigned to him.

In this parable, one went to work to discharge his duties. A second did the same. They did not have the same ability, but they worked with the same degree of faithfulness. The rewards were equal. The number of talents is not important. The thing that counts most is that we faithfully use what we have until Jesus comes and calls us to give account of our stewardship.

The parable of the pounds (Luke 19:11–26) teaches the same lesson, "Occupy till I come." These abilities are given us for a purpose—to use for God's glory. The man who buried his talent was not condemned for his lack of ability but for not using what he had. One who will bury one talent would bury a dozen if he had

81

them. We must be careful how we use or misuse talents. Faithfulness is the word. Stewardship does not mean possessions only but talents as well. We are stewards of everything we possess. God holds us responsible for the rightful use of all our gifts.

God Shows No Favoritism in Diversity of Gifts

"Well done," the master said to each faithful steward. God has so many places to fill and the things he wants done are so varied that he distributes his talents where they can be utilized best for his glory. There are no little places to fill, no insignificant things to be done in divine economy. Every place is important to him. Some parts of the body are small but no less important. The eye is small, but who will give up his eye for a foot or a leg? God has his own standard in computing success: not how many talents, but how faithful.

Every Talent Is Needed in Divine Economy

God needs skilled fingers. He needs keen and well-trained minds. Willing and ready feet make it possible for a dedicated voice to convey the message. In the building of a house or a church, there are ditches to dig, timbers to handle, brick to be laid, mortar to be mixed, but no one of these could make a building. All are important to the work of God. Nobody is a nobody. A one-talent man is as necessary as a ten-talent man.

The One-Talent Man Is Essential

Jesus spoke of a cup of cold water and its importance at the right place, at the right time. Never despise little or small things because Jesus does not. It was the one lost sheep, not a flock, that disturbed him and claimed his concern. Bank vaults with their millions were not his concern; it was the one small coin missing in the woman's house. It was not a congregation nor was it a family of which he spoke; it was one son, a prodigal. The big gift dropped into the offering plate did not get his attention; it was the widow's mite. How great and greatly to be praised is he for his concern for all of us.

Talents Multiply with Proper Use

"Give to him that used," said Jesus. The two talents and the five talents were doubled by proper use. It is God's purpose to multiply our talents if we use them with discretion for his glory. But talents left unused will be seized by paralysis. The owner will declare: "Let his opportunity cease. Take the talent from him and give it to the one with ten." The man that once had only five talents now had eleven.

The successful baseball pitcher gets his accuracy through practice. When I was young, I played baseball. I was encouraged to turn professional. But for thirty-five years I have not played baseball. What skill I had is gone now. Feed your capacity and it will grow; neglect it and it will die.

The Reckoning Day Is Certain

We must meet and account to the owner of the talents we have been given. The talents we misuse will be held against us in judgment. When Jesus returns, every knee shall bow. Everyone will be called into account, and the reckoning day will reveal the facts.

In that day one may say, "O Lord, our church did a marvelous work!" Then our Lord will ask, "Yes, but what part did you play in it?"

Another may say, "We have mission Sunday

Schools with large attendance, besides our school at the mother church." But our Lord will reply: "But what did you do? Where were you? How did you use your talents?"

This parable is personal. It means you; it means me. No one can be lost in the crowd. No one can account for another. Everyone must give account.

Men drive up to a church, put out their wives and children, and go on. These men have talents; God will hold them responsible. One day they will stand before the righteous Judge to give account of the talents they have. Do not neglect your duty, man. The time to correct these evils is now. Oh, Christian, will you not check on your condition and discover, before it is too late, what God expects of you?

Many who should be teaching classes are sitting on the sidelines in churches. They should be in the thick of the battle, yet they are looking on. Some who could sing in the choir sit in the balcony because they are too lazy to serve. Some who should be supporting the Lord's work occasionally tip God and still expect him to pour out his blessings upon them and their families.

What are you doing with that which God has given to you? Some use God's talents wisely; others misuse them. The day of reckoning is coming. It is a sin to misuse God's talents.

It is not a question of what the church is doing, nor is it what others are doing. The question is, What are you doing? Do not wrap God's precious talents in a napkin.

Misuse of Talents to Be Punished

The return of our Lord will be a great event for some but a sad disappointment for others. Jesus called the one-talent man who buried his talent "slothful," "unprofitable," "wicked." He said, " ' "Cast the worthless servant into the outer darkness" ' " (Matt. 25:29, RSV)—the court outside where spectators came to watch the feasts of the king. The servant had been unfaithful to his lord.

Jesus will patiently endure being misunderstood and even misrepresented, but he will not endure the misuse of his talents. He will not tolerate their lying waste.

Pride caused the unfaithful servant to hide his talent. He felt that he had been given an assignment too large for his ability. He refused to acknowledge his need of help. As a result, he became afraid.

Use the Talents God Has Given You

Some say, "Oh, if I could sing like that, I would be in the choir." Others say, "I would teach if I could." Do what you can with the talents you have, and you will be happy. God does not expect you to do more than he has endowed you to do. More people are misusing their talents than are using them for God's glory. Rewards will be according to faithfulness and not ability. If I do the best I can with what I have for Jesus' sake, that is enough. When we do our best, we need not worry.

Years ago the people of the church of a young man who felt God's call to preach gathered and sold their corn to send him to college. Some thought it a waste of money on John, but others believed in him. Later God sent John Claugh to China as a missionary. From his missionary efforts more than two thousand people were baptized. Those who helped John get his education and prayed for him will share in the rewards of his success in China. What if those farmers had

85

not put to use the talents God gave them? When we find God's will for using that with which we have been endowed, we shall hear his, "Well done." What more could we want?

9 Resources: Use Them Wisely

"This night thy soul shall be required of thee: then whose shall those things be?" (Luke 12:20).

"We plan to give Christ and his church first place in our lives just as soon as we get ahead," was the answer Tim and Rita gave their pastor as he sought constantly to enlist them in faithful service and devotion to their Lord through his church. Through hard work and skillful management, this young couple finally "got ahead." By neglecting their church and their spiritual lives with seven days of hard work every week, Tim and Rita acquired a tract of land and built a beautiful home, after which, they had promised their pastor, they would renew their vows to the Lord.

Without warning, a fatal disease hit Rita.

Within three days she was dead. The pastor was called upon to preach the funeral. The new home for which they had sacrificed their spiritual lives was so nearly completed that her body was taken there for the funeral.

Jesus is aware of the temptation of a covetous heart for young and old alike. He warns that many lay up for themselves treasures on earth and are not rich toward God. These people graduate in every class and live in every neighborhood. They are consulted in important business matters. We honor them with high positions, yet God calls them fools.

"And he thought within himself, saying, What shall I do, because I have no room where to bestow my fruits? And he said, This will I do: I will pull down my barns, and build greater; and there will I bestow all my fruits and my goods. And I will say to my soul, Soul, thou hast much goods laid up for many years; take thine ease, eat, drink, and be merry" (Luke 12:17–19).

Perhaps Jesus had just concluded a message on eternal life. He was interrupted by a man with an impossible request. Jesus did not take sides with the man who made the request or his brother who had the inheritance, but he had a message for both of them. He turned to them with the parable of the rich fool. In this parable Jesus exposed the sin of covetousness.

Commendable Qualities in the Man

1. He Was Rich and Prosperous

Jesus identified the man in his parable as a rich man. He said, "The ground of a certain rich man brought forth plentifully" (Luke 12:16). The man had a good farm. He evidently was a shrewd manager and a good worker. His land brought forth plentifully. No doubt he saved his money. Jesus did not condemn him for his ability to prosper and make money.

2. He Made His Money Honestly

Jesus did not criticize the man for the way he gained his possessions. Before his children entered the Promised Land, God reminded them that it was he who gave them power to get wealth (see Deut. 8:18). It was God who had blessed the man's efforts and had given him the increase.

Mistakes the Man Made

One may list a dozen good things about a person, then say "but," and erase all the good things said.

1. The Rich Man Left God Out of His Life

The rich fool had no consideration for God. He gave no thought to his soul. When time came for him to make a decision, Jesus said, "He counseled within himself." This is always a mistake, and all too many make it.

Not only did he ignore God, but he gave no consideration to his responsibility to others. He seemed to have no idea that God had a claim on his possessions. Little did he think that "the cattle upon a thousand hills" belong to God (Ps. 50:10), and that "the earth is the Lord's, and the fulness thereof; the world, and they that dwell therein" (Ps. 24:1). If anyone explained to the foolish man that God said, "Thy silver and thy gold is mine" (1 Kings 20:3), he paid no heed. From every indication, the man was a selfish, self-centered soul.

2. He Counseled Only with Himself

When he was certain that he had a bumper crop on his farm, he had a conference with himself. He thought, My barns are already full. What shall I do? When people fail to consult God and think only within themselves, they always make this sad mistake. Had this man taken God's advice, he would have been saved from this folly. The King James Version records the man's message to himself in sixty-one words. His key words are "I" and "my."

3. He Made Things His God

While the rich man lived, he failed to prepare to die. He let things master him. Possessions that belonged to God became his god.

4. He Decided to Keep All He Could

The conclusion reached by those who consult self is only to tear down their old barns and build bigger ones. They take no thought of the storehouses of God through which it is possible to lay up treasures in heaven. It is a tragic mistake for a man to say to his soul, "Take thine ease, thou hast plenty laid up; eat, drink, and be merry."

The Tragic Outcome

1. He Faced the God He Had Rejected

To this man and all like him, the verdict of Jesus is, "Thou fool." Imagine this prosperous egotist basking in the pleasures of plenty, suddenly facing the judgment of a righteous God. The dreams and selfish ambitions of his life crumble in upon him like a house built upon the sand. The finger of God wrote his doom upon the wall of time. "Thou fool, this night thy soul shall be required of thee: then whose shall those things be?" (Luke 12:20).

2. He Lost the Things He Worshiped

If his grave clothes had had pockets and if his friends had put his precious possessions in the tomb with him, the place to which he went would not have offered him opportunity to enjoy "these things." Often when a man dies, someone asks, "How much did he leave?" The answer always is, "He left it all."

3. A Lesson for the Covetous

Jesus nowhere put a premium on poverty, but he did issue warnings against the influence "much goods" may have on character. He taught that life does not consist in the abundance of things. Children able to say with the psalmist, "I have a goodly heritage" (Ps. 16:6) are not those whose parents leave them material possessions but those whose parents, through Christian living, teach them to love and trust Christ as Savior and Lord. It is far better to leave the memory of God-loving, God-fearing, and God-honoring parents than the fruits of a wasted life of covetousness.

When the king of Babylon had climbed to the top rung of the ladder to which material possessions can take a man, he said, "Is not this great Babylon that I have built for the house of my kingdom by the might of my power, and the honor of my majesty?" The God of Israel, who neither slumbers nor sleeps, happened to be listening to the foolish king. As was the case with the rich fool in the parable, God said to the selfish, self-centered, egotistical king, "O king Nebuchadnezzar, to thee it is spoken; The kingdom is departed from thee" (Dan. 4:31). The judgment of God upon the sin and folly of the covetous king was immediately set in action.

Covetousness takes its place in the Commandments of God along with theft, murder, and slander. Paul places it in the category with immorality, drunkenness, and other vile sins. Covetousness sits in church pews with head up, respected and unafraid.

In closing this parable, Jesus gave a miniature word picture of a fool: "He that layeth up   91 treasure for himself, and is not rich toward God" (Luke 12:21). Men who make prosperity speeches, even to themselves, should make sure they are equally rich spiritually.

Jesus looked upon the rich young ruler and loved him. He did not condemn him for his wealth. The Bible teaches that it is the love of money, not money itself, that is the root of all evil.

The Bible refers to prayer five hundred or more times and to faith less than that, but it refers to material possessions more than one thousand times. Of his thirty-eight parables, Jesus concerned himself in sixteen with stewardship of material possessions.

Conclusions

1. All things belong to God. The psalmist said, "The earth is the Lord's, and the fulness thereof; the world, and they that dwell therein" (Ps. 24:1).

2. The possession of wealth and the ability to accumulate it must be regarded as a stewardship, and men are responsible as stewards. "Moreover it is required in stewards, that a man be found faithful" (1 Cor. 4:2). A good steward will honor God with his possessions. God's Word says, "Honor the Lord with thy substance, and with the firstfruits of all thine increase: so shall thy barns be filled with plenty, and thy presses shall burst out with new wine" (Prov. 3:9–10).

3. The man who makes business his king will make gold his god. God said, "Thou shalt have no other gods before me" (Ex. 20:3).

4. The Bible teaches, "A good name is rather to be chosen than great riches, and loving favour than silver and gold" (Prov. 22:1).

5. God offers a partnership to man. For this

to be real, man must put God first.

6. If man would guard against the sin of covetousness, he must accept some scriptural principles of giving. "Every man according as he purposeth in his heart, so let him give; not grudgingly, or of necessity: for God loveth a cheerful giver" (2 Cor. 9:7). Jesus said: "Give, and it shall be given unto you; good measure, pressed down, and shaken together, and running over, shall men give into your bosom. For with the same measure that ye mete withal it shall be measured to you again" (Luke 6:38).

Again Jesus said, "But when thou doest alms, let not thy left hand know what thy right hand doeth: that thine alms may be in secret: and thy Father which seeth in secret himself shall reward thee openly" (Matt. 6:3–4).

Paul expressed it this way: "But this I say, He which soweth sparingly shall reap also sparingly; and he which soweth bountifully shall reap also bountifully" (2 Cor. 9:6).

Giving should be systematic. "Upon the first day of the week let every one of you lay by him in store as God hath prospered him, that there be no gatherings when I come" (1 Cor. 16:2).

Giving should be proportionate. "And thou shalt keep the feast of weeks unto the Lord thy God with a tribute of a freewill offering of thine hand, which thou shalt give unto the Lord thy God, according as the Lord thy God hath blessed thee" (Deut. 16:10).

Foolish Belshazzar followed his father's mistakes. He gave no consideration to God, and the finger of God wrote his doom on the wall when the king was in his glory in his banquet hall. The finger wrote, "Thou art weighed in the balances, and art found wanting" (Dan. 5:27). "Thou fool, this night thy soul shall be required of thee"

(Luke 12:20).

God's patience was long-suffering with Pharaoh, but finally he angered the Eternal and God let him destroy himself. We may write his doom in these words, "Thou fool."

The ravens have neither storehouses nor barns, but God feeds them. The lilies toil not, neither do they spin, but God sees that they grow. If God clothes the grass, feeds the ravens, and makes the lilies grow, how much more will he give us that which we have need of if we "seek first the kingdom of God"? Let none of us wait until the handwriting is on the wall to stop and consider our ways.

10 Sorrow: If You Have It, Handle It

"There hath no temptation taken you but such
as is common to man: but God is faithful, who
will not suffer you to be tempted above that ye
are able; but will with the temptation also
make a way to escape, that ye may be able to
bear it" (1 Cor. 10:13).
"My brethren, count it all joy when ye fall into
divers temptations; knowing this, that the trying
of your faith worketh patience" (Jas. 1:2–3).

Trials are inevitable. Shadows fall across the pathway of every person. Clouds appear on every horizon. There is an old Spanish proverb: "There is no home anywhere but that sooner or later it has its hush." Rich and poor alike must bear their burdens of sorrow; they come to saint and sinner. Even our Lord was forced to cry, "My God, why?"

There are trials by day and by night. There are trials in the morning of life and trials in the eventime of life. There are trials of sorrow, persecution, doubt, bewilderment, anxiety, oppression, ignorance—trials of all kinds press upon our spirits and bewilder and terrify our souls.

But, "God is our refuge and strength, a very present help in trouble. Therefore will not we fear" (Ps. 46:1–2). Of course, this only applies to one who has Christ as Lord. There is no such promise or help for one who has spurned the Savior.

Trials Come to God's Children

"Whom the Lord loveth he chasteneth, and scourgeth every son whom he receiveth. If ye be without chastisement, . . . then are ye bastards, and not sons. Furthermore, we have had fathers of our flesh which corrected us, and we gave them reverence: shall we not much rather be in subjection unto the Father of spirits, and live?" (Heb. 12:6,8–9). Jesus said: "As many as I love, I rebuke and chasten" (Rev. 3:19). "In the world ye shall have tribulation: but be of good cheer; I have overcome the world" (John 16:33).

As we study the lives of great Bible characters, we find that none of them were exempt from the trials of life. The three greatest trials ever to come to man came to Job, to Abraham, and to Christ. The theme of the book of Job is the sufferings of the righteous. God revealed to the world through Job that here was a man who could not be turned from him.

Job, God's servant, lost his possessions, his family and loved ones, his health, and his good name among his friends. He lost almost everything one could lose except his faith in God. Yet his life was spared (Job 1:1–21). In the midst of his great tribulation, his best friends mocked him. His wife even suggested to Job that he curse God and die (Job 2:9). The Sabeans took away his oxen. The fire of the Lord burned his sheep. The Chaldeans took away his camels and his drivers. The whirlwind killed his children, and Satan touched his flesh. Yet in all this, he remained faithful to God.

One evening as Abraham sat under the oak in front of his tent in the quiet of the day, he heard a voice speaking to him. It was no strange voice, for Abraham had heard it before. In the long ago the same voice had spoken to him, telling him that his seed would be as numerous as the stars and that in him all nations of the earth would be blessed. This time it was not a voice to speak of blessings that Abraham had waited and hoped for but a voice that frustrated all his plans. The message was plain that he was to take his only son Isaac to Mount Moriah and offer him as a sacrifice. This was a death blow to Abraham's dreams. There were no stars by night, no sun by day for Abraham during the hours of preparation for the sacrifice of his son as a burnt offering. Appetite and sleep left the old man as he gathered the wood, the flint, the knife, and the thongs with which to bind the sacrifice.

As they journeyed, Isaac asked his father about the lamb. Abraham replied, "God will provide the lamb." Never before had such an altar been built. Abraham was a great altar builder. Wherever he went he built an altar, but this was a new experience for him—an altar on which to offer his son. Abraham was tested with his dearest possession, his son of promise. He stood the test well.

David was a man after God's own heart. As a poet, he was unexcelled. As a musician, there was none like him. As a soldier, he was superb. As an organizer, he was unequalled. He took the scattered, broken, disorganized tribes of the two kingdoms and united them into one great nation. He was a financial wizard, gathering most of the money that later went into Solomon's

Temple. Yet he had his troubles. There were some dark, sad days in his life. One look at the beautiful woman bathing herself started him toward defeat and ruin. What followed brought David to shame, sorrow, and disgrace. The trials came. The child died. His sins came home. He must reap what he had sown. His own son defied him. In all this, David did not go down in defeat. He found the way back. God was his answer.

Habakkuk, like Paul, at first kicked against the goad. It seems that the prophet was so engrossed in the events on earth that he lost sight of God's care and presence. He watched the wicked surround and outnumber the righteous. The ungodly were in the saddle. Habakkuk was baffled. The testing time of his life had come. God seemed to have forgotten him. He became critical and complained about God's indifference. Only after the watchtower experience, he understood. At last he was ready to give God the glory.

Why Trials Come

Jesus cried, "My God, why?" Who has not at some time cried out, "Why?"

1. The critics of Job insisted that trouble was a sign of God's displeasures. Only sin, they said, would bring such affliction. Jesus did not teach this (Luke 13:1-4).

2. The story of the blind man that Jesus healed at the pool of Siloam defies such false doctrine. "Neither hath this man sinned, nor his parents," said Jesus, "but that the works of God should be made manifest in him" (John 9:3). Trouble, if rightly used, enables one to honor God. Just as one is to use time, talent, or possessions for his glory, so one is to use the trust of trouble or affliction to honor him. Instead, many people meet trouble only to be defeated and

embittered. They refuse to put their trust in the Lord. They withhold from him the glory that should be his through the trust of suffering that has been committed to them. They will not rely upon his exceeding great promises.

3. To the man thirty-eight years with infirmity, Jesus said, "Sin no more, lest a worse thing come unto thee" (John 5:14). Trials *may* be because of sin.

4. Trials may be to test our faith, to burn out the dross, to try us in the furnace, to finish the product.

5. Trials may be a trust. A trial may be to glorify God or to conform us to the image of his Son.

How Christians Should Act in Trials

No troubles befall us for which there is not in God a remedy, if only we rise to receive it. There is victory in the hour of trouble for every Christian. Three times the apostle sought the Lord to remove the thorn from his flesh, each time to hear, "My grace is sufficient" (2 Cor. 12:9). Finally Paul came to complete peace and contentment. It was more than resignation for Paul. With him, it was the absolute consent of his soul to receive God's will without resistance or rebellion. When he accepted the thorn as a trust from God, the victory was won. Even though it was a messenger from Satan to buffet him, God used it to keep Paul humble.

Some people chafe and fume, fret and worry under life's affliction, not laying to heart the precious promises of God: "For our light affliction, which is but for a moment, worketh for us a far more exceeding and eternal weight of glory" (2 Cor. 4:17) ; "and we know that all things work together for good to them that love God, to them who are the called according to his purpose" (Rom. 8:28).

While B. B. McKinney was leading the singing in a revival in Ruston, Louisiana, he referred several times to a sister who had several sons overseas in the service. Yet she kept a song in her heart. A few years later, I learned the secret of her song. I visited this woman's home while preaching in her church. Her devotion to her family, her church, and her God was a thing of beauty. Her faithfulness to duty and responsibility assured me that deep in her heart she lived daily in the Master's strength. She lived in the promise, "All things work together for good to them that love God" (Rom. 8:28). She was not afraid to trust God.

Tragedy struck two close friends of mine. When the first lost his baby, he went down in defeat. He was a professed Christian. Yet when he walked by the body of his child, he said that he had nothing left for which he should live. He said, "God has been unfair."

The other, when suddenly the life was crushed from his six-year-old son by a huge truck, said that God had a reason. He would draw closer to God, and even though the price had been terrible, perhaps God would bring about a revival in the community. As my friend knelt in the presence of four ministers, he prayed that God would give him the strength he needed, and that those who were to sing and preach the funeral would say what might be necessary to bring revival. He prayed that the tragedy that had come his way might cause sinners to repent.

This man had a secret. He knew the God of peace. Unbelief says, "God has forsaken me." Faith says, "God is trying me."

When Job's trouble came, he said, "Though

he slay me, yet will I trust him" (Job 13:15). "The Lord gave, and the Lord hath taken away; blessed be the name of the Lord" (Job 1:21). And in a moment there was peace within. The victory had been won.

One may say, "You do not understand; my trouble is worse than that." Paul was no novice in facing trouble. He said that he had suffered the loss of all things. He had endured almost every affliction and trial known to man. All through life he suffered a thorn in the flesh, yet he kept a peaceful heart and could say, "Our light affliction, which is but for a moment, worketh for us a far more exceeding . . . glory" (2 Cor. 4:17).

Habakkuk, though baffled by the mysteries he faced, concluded that there was an explanation and he would find it. He went to that watchtower to wait for the explanation from God. It came and Habakkuk understood. If you are troubled about the unsolved mysteries of life, or if you are undergoing some trial, then go to the watchtower. Wait on God for help and strength. "They that wait upon the Lord shall renew their strength" (Isa. 40:31).

Asaph was flooded with problems. Difficulties seemed to crush him. His faith almost failed. He decided to go to the Temple, hoping to find relief. Read Psalm 73. There, he said that he was almost gone, but when he went into the sanctuary of the Lord, he understood.

Many of our trials, troubles, sorrows, heartaches, and doubts flee when we accept God's will for our lives and trust him to guide us over the rough places.

The Cure for Worry in Time of Trouble

1. Review your blessings. One of the best anti-

dotes for worry is to remember the times when God extended his mercy.

2. See the conditions of those who are worse off. Minister to the bereaved, the sick, and the needy. You will come away praising God for his goodness. Visit the hospitals. Hear the cries of the suffering and the parting words of the dying. You will rejoice in your light affliction that is only for a season. Remember the man who complained that he had no shoes until he saw a man who had no feet.

3. Fix your eyes on the distant goal. Declare with Abraham that you look for a city that has foundations, whose builder and maker is God. We are pilgrims here on earth, and we seek a country that God has prepared for us. The one who has gone ahead and mapped out the way has experienced all the testings of life that come our way. He has gone on and beckons us to come up higher.

4. The surest way to peace of heart when billows roll over you is complete submission to God's will. Jesus said, "My grace is sufficient for thee" (2 Cor. 12:9).

11 Love: You Have It; Share It

"There came unto him a woman having an alabaster box of very precious ointment, and poured it on his head, as he sat at meat" (*Matt. 26:7*).

At the invitation of Simon the leper, who was giving a supper in his honor, Jesus had come once again to the little town of Bethany. Evidently at one time Jesus had healed Simon of his leprosy, and to do something for him Simon decided to have a supper in Jesus' honor. In Bethany were three special friends of Jesus—Mary, Martha, and their brother Lazarus. They were invited to the house of Simon for this feast. Read the account in Matthew 26:6–13 and John 12:1–9.

Martha, Mary, and Lazarus, whom Jesus had restored to life, with others of the disciples were present for the feast. As they reclined at the table, Mary saw what the leper was doing to honor the one who had cleansed him of his leprosy. Evidently she decided that she must do something for Christ, who had not cleansed her of leprosy but had saved her from sin. He also had restored her brother Lazarus to life.

What could she do? Her alabaster box was the best she had. She took it and anointed Jesus with it. According to Judas, it was worth three hundred pence. Three hundred pence was a year's wages for the average worker. She brought the box of very precious oinment, according to Matthew, and poured it on Jesus' head. According to John, she anointed his feet. Jesus said, "She has poured this perfume on me to prepare my body for burial" (Matt. 26:12, TLB).[1]

One of the disciples, identified by John as Judas the betrayer, said: "Why the waste? Why did you not take this ointment and sell it and give it to the poor?" Jesus saw and understood what was taking place. He immediately came to Mary's rescue by saying: "Let her alone. She has wrought a good work on me." (See Matt. 26:8–10; Mark 14:6; John 12:7.) She had done what she could, with what she had, for Jesus' sake.

In this incident are four lessons: first, Jesus' concern for women; second, a woman's devotion to Jesus; third, the attitude of Judas; fourth, the time to do our best for Christ.

Jesus' Concern for Women
1. Man Condemns; Jesus Christ Forgives

Note how Jesus replied to the critics of Mary: "When Jesus understood it, he said unto them, Why trouble ye the woman? for she hath wrought

....
[1] From *The Living Bible, Paraphrased* (Wheaton: Tyndale House Publishers, 1971). Used by permission.

a good work upon me. . . . Wheresoever this
gospel shall be preached in the whole world,
there shall also this, that this woman hath done,
be told for a memorial of her" (Matt. 26:10–13).
These words reveal the gentleness, compassion,
and concern of Jesus for women. It is said that
God did not take woman from man's head to
rule over him, or from beneath his feet to be
trampled by him, but from under his arm, near
his heart, to be equal with and protected by him.

In countries where Jesus has not been introduced, women are used as servants by men.
Where Jesus has his way, women are lifted to
their rightful place in society. Before Christ was
introduced in India by missionaries, mothers
threw their babies to the crocodiles to appease
their gods. In other places of the heathen world,
women have been tied to the bodies of their
dead husbands and burned alive. This is true
no more where Jesus has been preached. Should
we not love him better, serve him more because
of his concern and compassion for women?

Where Christ has a chance, he lifts fallen
women. Remember the group that dragged the
sinful woman into the presence of Jesus? When
asked what could be done about it, Jesus stooped
to write in the sand. While he was writing in the
sand with his finger, the men left. When he
stood, he said to the guilty woman, "Where are
thine accusers?" She said, "No man is here to
accuse me, Lord." Jesus said, "Neither do I; go,
and sin no more." (See John 8:1–11.) Jesus
forgave her, and she went her way redeemed in
the precious blood of the Lord Jesus Christ.

After all he has done for women, how can
any woman refuse to love him with a pure heart,
serve him with a true devotion, and be loyal
to his cause? But not so! Some have rejected

his will for their lives. Some have trampled under foot his great concern, compassion, and love for them. Some have wasted their lives in riotous living and spurned the will of Christ. Yet Jesus reveals his genuine concern for them. He loves them still.

A Woman's Devotion to Jesus
1. Love Responds to Love

In Matthew 26 we read of a woman's devotion to Christ. John identifies this woman as Mary, the sister of Martha and Lazarus. According to him, the alabaster box contained a pound of pure nard. It was this that she poured on the body of our Lord.

A woman's devotion to Christ is beautiful to behold. It is marvelous to watch women dedicate themselves to the services and program of the Master. Some willingly give of their lives, their services, their talents, and their money. Women around the world have carried on the program of the Master when few men would give of their time and service. Women through the years have preached missions, given to missions, lived missions, and have gone out as missionaries to the ends of the earth, when others refused to help. Where would evangelism be today had it not been for the faithful stewardship of great women who kept the fires burning?

2. Love Spares Not

Why did Mary break the alabaster box? Why did she anoint the Lord? Why is a mother up through the night, seeing that the tiny babe is cozy in the crib? Why was Jesus willing to give up everything that was his with God the Father and come to earth, be tabernacled in the flesh for a season, dwell among men, and then go to the cross to die for us? Why did he do it? John 3:16

is the answer: "For God so loved the world, that he gave his only begotten Son, that whosoever believeth in him should not perish, but have everlasting life." One little word, *love!* God so loved! Why did this woman take all that she had, the treasure she had cherished, why did she break it? One word answers—*love!*

3. Love Breaks the Alabaster Box

Memories linger of women and men in many churches whose devotion and loyalty to Christ spur me to greater loyalty in service to my Lord. In one church where I was pastor, the time had come for us to enlarge. A new building was necessary if we were to reach the multitudes for Christ. As best I could, I appealed to the people to break their boxes, to anoint Christ afresh with what they had, to reveal their devotion to him who loved us and gave himself for us. I shall never forget when the invitation was given how they came down the aisles. A woman well over fifty placed something in my hand. As she did, she said, "This is all I have that I can call my own, but I want to give it to the building of a house of worship to the glory of Jesus."

When people are in the will of God, they are willing to anoint Christ with their best. The pound of pure nard was costly, but not too costly for this woman to give to Jesus. He was Mary's friend; she was his friend. He was her Savior; she crowned him as her Lord.

The Attitude of Judas

1. Attitudes Control Actions

"But when his disciples saw it, they had indignation, saying, To what purpose is this waste?" (Matt. 26:8). Begin anointing Jesus if you want to expose the Judases in your church. "This ointment might have been sold for much and given

107

to the poor," said Judas. (See Matt. 26:9.) We find this attitude in churches today. Never is an enlarged program launched in any church but that Judas reveals himself. Every time a church starts a building program, every time a program of enlargement is suggested, every time some expense is proposed to advance God's kingdom, Judas cannot stand it. He is sure to reveal himself. Pray for him.

2. The Attitude of Judas Must Not Prevail

God's work must go foward, regardless of Judas. We cannot afford to be sidetracked by such men and women. We cannot turn aside from the eternal will anl plan of God to satisfy any man who has not had an experience with the Lord or who has no vision of his responsibility for reaching the multitudes for Christ. If we are to witness to the last person on earth, our program must be enlarged and our vision broadened. We must not be hindered by Judas, even if he belongs to our church.

The Time to Anoint Christ Is Now

Jesus said, "For ye have the poor always with you; but me ye have not always" (Matt. 26:11). The time to do what we intend to do for Christ is now. We are not promised tomorrow. Now is the day of salvation; now is the accepted time. Today is the day of opportunity.

If you intend to anoint Christ, do it now. If you intend to do anything with your life for Jesus, do it now. For the lost, now is the time to be saved. For the Christian, now is the time to surrender to service. If God has called, then it is time to devote your life to service. It is time for your life to be given to Christ and his cause. It is time to preach the gospel of Christ, if he is calling you.

George Eliot tells of a man who left his wife and went West seeking gold. Years crept upon him and health failed. He still had not accomplished his purpose. He went back East seeking his wife. He went to the old homeplace where, years ago, he had left her. In response to his request the voice at the door said: "Millie was buried yesterday. The flowers are not wilted." To the graveside the man went. He stretched himself out over the flowers on the grave and cried, "O Millie, Millie, I did love you; can you hear me now?"

Millie could not hear him; it was too late. May God help us to break the alabaster box and anoint Christ with what we have, where we are, while we can, for Jesus' sake. Christians could take this nation for Christ if we would. We could take it now. Let us anoint Christ today.

12 What Your Church Expects from You

"And he gave some, apostles; and some, prophets; and some, evangelists; and some, pastors and teachers; for the perfecting of the saints, for the work of the ministry, for the edifying of the body of Christ" (Eph. 4:11–12).

Visitors find some puzzling areas in the desert of Arizona. On one side of the highway is barren desert, as dry, hard, and fruitless as the pavement on the road. On the other side of the road, the land yields four to five bales of cotton per acre. There is no difference in the soil. It is the same on both sides of the road. Irrigation makes the difference.

What irrigation does for the soil, the Holy Spirit does for the Christian. Add water to the fertile soil of the desert and harvest is sure. When the Holy Spirit controls, the believer is fruitful. God expects his church to be the agency through which his children dedicate, and use, their abilities.

Some churches grow and reach people while others bear no fruit. It is the God-given task of a New Testament church to reach people. Where there are people, churches can and should reach them. When, under similar circumstances, one church reaches people and another does not, there must be a reason. Churches desiring to reach people should find the answer.

Some churches seem content not to reach people. They must have decided that outreach cannot be done in their situation. Churches not reaching people should examine the purpose, plan, and results that motivate their activities. The Holy Spirit could be limited by the congregation or leadership of their church. The Holy Spirit can make the difference.

Failure to reach people in a church involves both leadership and followship. Either or both may be to blame for not reaching people. Basics are never discovered by some people. Others fail to reach people because of undedicated followers. "Not by might, nor by power, but by my spirit, saith the Lord of hosts" (Zech. 4:6). Our labors are in vain unless the indwelling Holy Spirit is in control.

Your Church Provides a Place of Service

A New Testament church is an organism; yet if this organism is not well organized, it is a monstrosity. When properly organized, a church distributes responsibility and spells out each task.

1. The Purpose of Your Church

To understand the purpose of a church, read Paul's statements: "And he gave some, apostles; and some, prophets; and some, evangelists; and some, pastors and teachers; for the perfecting of the saints, for the work of the ministry, for the edifying of the body of Christ; till we all come in the unity of the faith, and of the knowledge of the Son of God, unto a perfect man, unto the measure of the stature of the fulness of Christ" (Eph. 4:11–13).

God had a purpose for the home when he established it; Jesus had a purpose for his church when he founded it. There are long-range and short-range objectives of a church. No one knew these objectives better than the church's founder. He, the head and sustainer of his church, has a right to decide its basic purposes. He said to his disciples, "I will build my church; and the gates of hell shall not prevail against it. And I will give unto thee the keys . . . and whatsoever thou shalt bind on earth shall be bound in heaven: and whatsoever thou shalt loose on earth shall be loosed in heaven" (Matt. 16:18–19).

A New Testament church is of people, by people, and for people. When it fails to reach people and meet their spiritual needs, it fails in its purpose. The local assembly has no authority to change the basic purpose for which Jesus instituted his church. No group outside or any individual inside has any right to alter the divinely given program of a church. When the Holy Spirit generates compassion for souls, churches reach people. He does this through individuals who dethrone self and enthrone Jesus Christ in their lives.

2. The Function of Your Church

According to the Scriptures, the major function of a New Testament church is to reach people. Jesus spent his earthly ministry doing this. He died that we might work at the ministry of reconciliation between a just and righteous

God and lost, estranged people. To this end the Holy Spirit distributes various abilities to believers.

Many and varied are the ideas about the function of a church. The Holy Spirit gives the correct answer through the New Testament. When Jesus said, "I will build my church," he did not mean a building of wood or stone. Buildings, like organization, are means to an end. At least ninety-three times in the New Testament the term "church" refers to a local group. About thirteen times the term is used in a general sense. A New Testament church is a company of people living on earth. A church is a local assembly of "called out ones," each having trusted Jesus Christ as Lord and Savior and having been regenerated, scripturally baptized, and joined together as a body of believers in Christ, to carry out his commands set forth in the Great Commission. (See Matt. 28:19-20.) The Holy Spirit indwells each believer and accomplishes God's purpose as these believers yield to his will.

Jesus knew that some would be confused about the term "church." The Bible contains many figures of speech to indicate the true function of a church. A church is spoken of as a lampstand. Lampstands give no light, but when used properly, they hold forth the light. The church is not a light, but it holds forth the Light, Christ Jesus. The church is to lift up Jesus who is the Light of the world. (See John 8:12.)

The "body of Christ" is used to identify the church. (See 1 Cor. 12:27.) Another beautiful picture of a church is the "bride of Christ." "The Spirit and the bride say, Come" (Rev. 22:17). This figure magnifies reaching people, the basic purpose of a church. The "household of faith"

113

suggests reaching people as the business of a church.

Simon Peter spoke of a New Testament church as a "spiritual house" made of living stones. (See 1 Pet. 2:4–5.) Paul spoke of it as "God's building." (See 1 Cor. 3:9.) How could one misunderstand such graphic language? All these figures of speech involve people.

Through the Bible and the leadership of the Holy Spirit, Christians can know the will of God. The challenging command of our Lord is, "Go ye therefore, and make disciples" (Matt. 28:19, ASV). The world is fast decaying. Jesus told his followers that they were the salt to stop the decaying.

The world in which we live is dark. Jesus is the Light of the world. The church is the lampstand. We are to hold forth this Light. Jesus said, "And I, if I be lifted up from the earth, will draw all men unto me" (John 12:32). When we lift up Jesus, he will light the world.

The church has the only gospel that will cure the world's ills. The gospel of redemption, through the shed blood of Christ, is what the world needs. Churches are charged with the responsibility of giving this message to the world. This message, in the power of the Holy Spirit, will reach people.

3. The Program of Your Church

A New Testament church not only has a purpose and a function, it also has a program. Jesus organized a local church, but he gave it a worldwide task. Jesus believed in people. He took what he could get and made them to become what he wanted them to be. Jesus presented a challenge that led people to be willing to lay down their lives if need be. Unlike the rabbi, the shepherds, and the wise men, Jesus was

114

perfectly at home with common people. He did not hesitate to ask people to do things. He knew how to motivate people. Jesus loved the unlovely. He loved little children and gave consideration to them. A church cannot do everything that Jesus did, but it can and must address itself to these things Jesus commanded the church to do.

Jesus Christ assigned the church its task. It includes preaching, teaching, witnessing, enlisting, training, activating, and motivating.

"It is as important to save what we have as it is to save the lost," a leader has said. This was the emphasis of Jesus: "Teaching them to observe all things whatsoever I have commanded you: and, lo, I am with you alway, even unto the end of the world" (Matt. 28:20). If this had been the conviction of Southern Baptists through the years, the more than two million members now lost to the cause could be active.

The late L. R. Scarborough, president of Southwestern Baptist Theological Seminary, often told students, "One hundred new converts are one hundred liabilities until they are assimilated into the life of a church." Many soul-winning pastors have to move on to another field because they are not as capable in assimilating new members as they are in winning them.

Jesus said, "Lo, I am with you alway," after he said, "Teaching them to observe all things whatsoever I have commanded you." Why will some pastors and evangelists allow themselves to master on one phase of evangelism and be a complete failure at the other? Evangelism that turns a new convert loose before he becomes an evangelist is incomplete.

Suppose that a mother, after giving birth to a baby, felt that her responsibility was over. The baby would be helpless. He would have been better off never to have been born. A church is to be responsible for its members. Just as a new baby in a home brings added responsibilities to parents, new members bring added joy and responsibilities to a church. New converts should be enlisted immediately in the life and work of the church. Every church organization should feel responsible for the enlistment of every talent of every new member. Until this is done, new members will be liabilities rather than assets.

The Sunday School should spearhead the outreach of a church, but it is the duty of other church organizations to help enlist, educate, and activate members after they are reached, saved, and united with the church.

Every newborn babe in Christ should leave the baptismal waters to "walk in newness of life." It becomes the responsibility of Church Training, Sunday School, Woman's Missionary Union, Brotherhood, and Church Music to help make it possible for a new convert to "walk in newness of life." Failure of any one of these organizations to help do this leaves it without a reason to exist.

A church uses or loses new members at this point. The late J. E. Lambdin, "Mr. Training Union," often said, "The most tragic human figure on earth is an indifferent, undeveloped, unenlisted, sinning Christian." Was he not right? Why do we have so many like this? Has the Sunday School failed? Is it failure on the part of Church Training, Brotherhood, or Woman's Missionary Union? It could be failure by all of these.

The pastor who acquaints himself with the valuable helps of church organizations in assimilating new members and in using them can have an asset in every new member; otherwise, each new member is a liability. New converts are no more responsible for added problems to a church than a new baby is responsible for problems in the home.

Three churches of my experience had as their slogan, "Every Member Saved and Serving." They added to that, "Enlist or Dismiss." Any member who refused to be enlisted in the activity of the church disqualified himself for membership in that church.

A New Testament church has a right to expect its members to attend the services. The writer to the Hebrews said, "Not forsaking the assembling of ourselves together, as the manner of some is" (Heb. 10:25). Unless providentially hindered, church members ought to attend the services of their church. It is not unreasonable for a church to expect her members to walk orderly before God and men (1 Cor. 5:13; 2 Cor. 6:17; Matt. 18:15–18; Rev. 2:12–17).

A New Testament church has a right to expect every member to support the church, not only with attendance and service but financially. Paul said, "Now concerning the collection . . . . Upon the first day of the week let every one of you lay by him in store, as God has prospered him, that there be no gatherings when I come" (1 Cor. 16:1–2). He also said, "Therefore, as ye abound in every thing, in faith, and utterance, and knowledge, and in all diligence, and in your love to us, see that ye abound in this grace also" (2 Cor. 8:7).

The amount of one's financial support is not as important as the spirit in which it is given. "For if there be first a willing mind, it is accepted according to that a man hath, and not according to that he hath not" (2 Cor. 8:12).

It is important that people know the will of God concerning the support of their church. "But this I say, He which soweth sparingly shall reap also sparingly; and he which soweth bountifully shall reap also bountifully" (2 Cor. 9:6).

Since the church is responsible for its member's spiritual and physical welfare, some churches support any member who is unable to help bear the financial load of the church. Any member who cannot help support the church may need the church's support. Paul said: "Brethren, if a man be overtaken in a fault, ye which are spiritual, restore such an one in the spirit of meekness; considering thyself, lest thou also be tempted. Bear ye one another's burdens, and so fulfil the law of Christ" (Gal. 6:1–2).

The goal of every church should be a regenerated membership, a separated membership, and a compassionate membership. Paul said, "If any man be in Christ, he is a new creature" (2 Cor. 5:17). He said, "Come out from among them, and be ye separate, saith the Lord" (2 Cor. 6:17). John said, "Love not the world, neither the things that are in the world" (1 John 2:15). Paul said, "There is therefore now no condemnation to them which are in Christ Jesus, who walk not after the flesh, but after the Spirit" (Rom. 8:1).

As a pastor for twenty-two years, I have found no difficulty in enlisting church members. A helpful practice has made this possible. Every organization had its specific assignment with a well-defined job description. Each organization is expected to carry its responsibility in enlisting members.

In addition to this, the church membership is divided into groups of twenty-five or less families. A deacon is made spiritual leader of each group. The assignment is given him by the church. Members of his group know that he is their spiritual leader and helper. It is his duty to enlist all members of the families of his group in at least three church activities: first, in attendance at the services of the church; second, in Christian conduct; and third, in financial support of the church. The members of the church understand this to be a part of the church program.

Each deacon may call upon any member of his group to assist him in enlisting members in these activities. After three months if any deacon has members of his group who have not been enlisted in some phase of church life, he exchanges such members with another deacon who works with these unenlisted members for another three months, doing everything possible to enlist them in the work of the church. If this deacon and his group fail to make progress with a member during the next three months, then the pastor is assigned the responsibility for an additional three months.

At the beginning of this program, the church adopted a policy that if at the end of this period any member could not be enlisted, he would be brought before the church. Then he was given an additional three months, making a full year, to decide whether he would be enlisted or dismissed.

The church voted for the pastor to mail letters to all families of the church at the end of each month, indicating the progress of the church for the past month, announcing the activities of the church for the coming month, and a financial report of the church for the past month. The letter closed with a statement like this: "Our records show that you gave $_____ for the month." Every name of every member of the family was listed in the letter, and the blank space was filled in with the exact amount given by each member of each family. If there had been no gift from any member of the family, a zero was placed in the blank.

It was amazing what this letter did in enlisting people in regular attendance and in systematic giving to their church. In one of the three churches where this procedure was followed, the number of systematic givers increased from 390 to 1,100 in less than a year's time, and the number of people attending Bible study increased from 865 to 1,665 in three years.

Churches are responsible if members are not activated. Where the right spirit prevails and the proper motive for enlistment is evident, churches have no serious problem in enlisting blood-bought, sin-forgiven people in full support of the church program.

This was only a part of the enlistment program of these churches. In addition to the deacons in a church, there may be hundreds of other leaders in the Sunday School, Church Training, the Woman's Missionary Union, the Brotherhood, the Church Music, and other activities of the church. Without the help of these leaders, the deacons of these churches never could have produced the results cited.

Hindrances to the Lord's Work

After studying all the religions of the world and reading carefully through the Bible, Gandhi, former prime minister of India, said, "I would embrace Christianity if I had not known some Christians."

The man who set off Hitler's ambition, said, "I will believe in these Christians' Redeemer when I can see evidence of Him in them."

Over the door of a women's Sunday School class was the word "Inseparable." It was impossible to get a worker from that class, for they were not interested in reaching more women. They were happy. They said: "This is our room. We put covers on these chairs. We put that air conditioner in the window. We painted these walls. We enjoy a wonderful fellowship. Our class is large enough. There is not a lost person in it. What better could we have? Let us alone."

While the ninety-nine play church, hell enlarges. The ninety-nine church members ought to be mobilized to reach the one lost person. Instead, in some churches the ninety-nine are "at ease in Zion." Christ is dishonored, people are not reached, and the Holy One of Israel is limited. Yet the ninety-nine seem happy and content. What has happened? Why is there such unconcern? Where is the compassion for the "lost sheep" that once we had?

1. Unchristian Conduct

Shabby living on the part of professed Christians hinders the progress of the gospel. Unchristian conduct dishonors Christ. It disgusts lost people and causes the witness of the church to lose its power. Choir members who stand and sing Sunday after Sunday with unconfessed sin in their lives do not win people to Christ with their testimony in song. The Sunday School teacher who is seen in questionable places does not have the influence that he should. The deacon who makes crooked business deals loses his influence. Workers who criticize the church program have no weight. Compassion for souls is no companion to secret sins. When part of the body is unfit, the whole is hindered. Unchristian conduct in the lives of church members causes the unsaved to be at ease in their sins.

2. Lack of Compassion

Hungry people claimed the attention of Jesus, but lost people moved him to compassion. Jesus restored sight to the blind, but it was the spiritual blindness of the multitudes that moved him to compassion. Lepers sought help from Jesus and he made them whole, yet Jesus did not get upset because men had leprosy. It was cancer of the soul that moved Jesus to compassion. Physical death could not remain in the presence of the Son of God. He restored the dead to life. But it was not separation of the soul from the body that brought Jesus to compassion; it was separation of a soul from God. When he saw the multitudes scattered as sheep without a shepherd, it broke his heart. Unconcern of pastor or people brings hurt to the cause.

Concern for people is not found in the soil of complacency. Unconcern of Christians within the church hinders a successful program of outreach for the unreached. The church with a wide-awake, forward-moving, evangelistic spirit, produced by people moved with compassion for the multitudes, can overcome the unconcern of some members. The resurrected Lord spoke harsh words of rebuke to the church at Laodicea. (See Rev. 3:15–17.) Unconcern, indifference, and complaceny had taken possession of the people of Laodicea. This hurts the cause of Christ. This hinders a church in its outreach for new people. Churches not reaching new people should examine their purpose and program.

3. Jealousy

A cold heart and a jealous spirit in a church can kill evangelistic fervor. Clamoring for recognition, seeking credit, asking for more attention can be the ruin of a church program of reaching people. Dissatisfied, disgruntled church members hinder the zeal of a church. Many people who should be after souls, bringing them to Christ, hinder those who want to be soul-winners. Friction among members hurts the progress of a church and dishonors our Lord.

4. Wrong Attitudes

The Bible is hard on people with the wrong spirit. We are admonished to have in us the mind that is in Christ. If the Spirit of Christ dwells in us, he makes the difference. Some of us may be limited in our abilities, our talents may be few, but we can have a warm spirit. There is room at the top for many like this.

5. Misplaced Love

Many Christian workers may need to take the test that Jesus gave Simon Peter when he asked, "Simon, son of Jonas, lovest thou me more than these?" (John 21:15).

When we settle the love question for Jesus Christ, other things fall into proper perspective. When people get right on the Son question, they become right on the sin question. The money question is settled for those who love Jesus with all their hearts. Our service, our allegiance, our devotion all belong to Jesus, and we will not withhold it from him when our love for him is sure.

The lost world becomes our field when we truly love our Lord. The two million Baptists that are lost to the cause would all join the church nearest them next Sunday if they truly loved Christ. Misplaced love in the membership of a church hinders reaching people.

6. Lack of Vision

The Bible says, "Where there is no vision, the people perish" (Prov. 29:18). Churches should grow. Leaders must believe this. Southern Baptist churches should be reaching more people. To see the multitudes through the eyes of Jesus Christ would awaken many to the golden opportunity for reaching people. Possibly our prayer should be, "Lord, open our eyes that we may see."

The blind cannot lead the blind. Those who assume leadership roles should stay out beyond the people they lead in seeking the will of God for his church. The group following the apostle Paul made no attempt to go around his leadership. They waited for his vision. He was never short on vision; he was keenly sensitive to the will and leadership of God. His followers knew this well. "Immediately we endeavoured to go into Macedonia, assuredly gathering that the Lord had called us for to preach the gospel unto them" (Acts 16:10). This is as it should be, yet many churches are waiting upon their leader to lead them.

7. Cares of This World

In the heart of every Christian there comes a desire to be a soul-winner. Things crowd out this desire. Many church people have exchanged compassion for people for concern for things. There are too many places to go, too many things to see, and too many meetings to attend. Perhaps all of these are good, but when Christians get too busy to reach additional people for the Lord, they are too busy.

8. Lack of Responsibility

Before church members accept their responsibility to reach new people, they must be brought face to face with their God-given mission. They must see that "this is my task." Saved people are charged with this responsibility. Church leaders are responsible to lay this burden upon the hearts of the people.

124   9. Anemic Faith

Habakkuk, a noble prophet of God, allowed his faith to become so faint that his leadership ability was like the blind leading the blind. Before this tragic situation became disgraceful, God persuaded Habakkuk to climb to the watchtower and seek once again the presence and will of God.

God expects his leaders to be strong in faith. A Christian leader always must manifest implicit faith in God. When this is not true, God is dishonored and his cause is hindered. Jeremiah asked, "Righteous art thou, O Lord, when I plead with thee: yet let me talk with thee of they judgments: Wherefore doth the way of the wicked prosper?" (Jer. 12:1). Asaph said, "Behold, these are the ungodly, who prosper in the world; they increase in riches" (Ps. 73:12). Asaph concluded that God is good to those who are upright. Is it any wonder many people see no reason to follow Christ? God's leaders must have a constant, dynamic faith and always demonstrate it.

10. Major on Minors

Too often leaders allow the good to become the enemy of the best. It has become increasingly harder through the years to reach people. Every leader finds his hands full; things overwhelm him. Unless prayerfully alert, a leader may be like a king of old, of whom the prophet of God said, "As thy servant was busy here and there, he [the man] was gone" (1 Kings 20:40).

Leaders must plan carefully to make sure their efforts are spent doing the main thing—reaching people.

11. Piddlers Instead of Preachers

Preachers should preach. The prophets preached. Jesus preached. When people heard him, they were amazed. The apostle said, "We will give ourselves continually to prayer, and

125

to the ministry of the word" (Acts 6:4).

When a preacher leaves a field, it ought to be a sad day for the people. Every preacher should live so that the people identify him as God's man in their midst. When Elijah was taken up from the presence of the people, Elisha stood weeping, saying, "There goes the defense of Israel." What a man Elijah was, what an example!

God pronounced a curse upon the leaders of the children of Israel during Malachi's day because they treated lightly the commandments of God "I will curse your blessings . . . because ye do not lay it to heart" (Mal. 2:2). "For the priest's [minister's] lips should keep knowledge, and they should seek the law at his mouth: for he is the messenger of the Lord of hosts" (Mal. 2:7).

The pastor's job is unique. God promises protection and blessings to his called servants who are faithful; but one who limits God and one who is partial in the law, who does not keep all his ways, he makes contemptible and base before all the people. It is dangerous for a God-called leader to limit the Holy One of Israel.

Some Christian leaders have been accused of carelessness and deceitfulness in the work of the Lord. This God does not allow to go unnoticed. He said, "Cursed be he that doeth the work of the Lord deceitfully" (Jer. 48:10).

Twentieth-century Christians playing church should take seriously God's word spoken by Malachi: "Who is there even among you that would shut the doors for nought? neither do ye kindle fire on mine altar for nought. I have no pleasure in you, saith the Lord of hosts, neither will I accept an offering at your hand" (Mal. 1:10). It is time to repent and do the first works referred to in Revelation 2:5.

Teaching Suggestions

James Cartwright

General Preparations

1. Read this book; urge study participants to read it also.
2. Plan adequate teaching time. Consider these alternatives:
   (1) Monday, Tuesday, Thursday—Two 65-minute periods, plus a 15-minute break, each evening; Wednesday—One 60-minute period, followed by regular midweek prayer service.
   (2) Monday, Tuesday, Thursday, Friday—Two 60-minute periods, plus a 15-minute break, each evening.
   (3) On one day, Saturday, plan a "Stewardship Blitz" of seven and one-half hours. Start with a light breakfast, serve a light lunch, and conclude in the afternoon.
   (4) Plan an eight-week study in the regular, ongoing Adult and/or Youth Church Training groups.
3. Plan for special arrangements:
   (1) Plan to have the participants seated around tables, if possible, or in a circle with small lapboards (for writing).
   (2) Plan for such child care as is needed and possible.
4. Plan and secure resources needed:
   (1) Urge the participants to bring their personal Bibles for each session.
   (2) Research the information needed for duplicating in session 1, chapter 3, action 3. Allow ample time for the church staff to fit this into their schedule. Action 4

of chapter 3 requires postcards for participants to use as a follow-through on action 3.

(3) Provide copies of the tract "A Full and Meaningful Life."

(4) Provide copies of the church's current or projected budget.

(5) Ask someone to do the research called for in session 4, chapter 10, action 2.

(6) Have copies of your church covenant or of *Baptist Hymnal* available for the session 4 action relative to the church covenant.

Session Plans

SESSION 1

Chapter 1: Your Christian Life Is on Display

Action 1.—Divide into groups of threes and, using the King James Version of the Bible, write the Hebrews 11 scene in the everyday language of the group.

Action 2.—Have a youth athlete (or adult who was a former athlete) describe an athletic training camp, how athletes get ready for sports competition. Invite the participants to discuss the meaning of discipline for Christian training.

Action 3.—List some disciplines needed in the Christian life for daily victorious Christian living (that is, prayer, Bible study, worship, giving, witness, commitment, training), and list ways these disciplines can be accomplished.

Action 4.—Discuss the following disciplines of prayer: meditation on God's Word, conversation with God, emergency prayer, spontaneous prayer, thankfulness, joy. Discuss the best time for prayer. Call for volunteers to tell why they chose their particular time.

Chapter 2: Gods' Plan Is for You; Accept It

Action 1.—Ask participants to write a definition of God's will.

Action 2.—Suggest three expressions of God's will: his ideal will, his circumstantial will, his permissive will. Ask for illustrations of each. These three concepts are a feature of *The Will of God* by Leslie Weatherhead. Although the whole of Weatherhead's book will not be useful in the study, use these three concepts of God's will. Invite a testimony of God's permissive will. Ask, Why is God permissive? (His gift of choice to men is real.) Invite a testimony of God's circumstantial will. ("God used me to do . . . in spite of my personal limitations.") Ask, Why does God use people where he finds them? (His grace does not require us to be perfect to be used.) Ask, Why are so few in God's ideal will?

Action 3.—Discuss how God's will is determined. (Inner testimony of the Holy Spirit, gifts of the Holy Spirit—at least, potential gifts, recognition by the church, evaluation of past experiences, and so on.)

Action 4.—Discuss the characteristics of God's will in Romans 12:1–2 (good; acceptable; perfect, or mature, or complete).

Chapter 3: You Duty to God and Country

Action 1.—Ask the group to discuss freely the question, When does one become a citizen of God's kingdom? (Col. 1:12–14).

Action 2.—Plan a debate: *"Resolved,* That the highest loyalty is to one's country." Use several participants to take both sides. Limit each

to five minutes' preparation (while others work
on action 3) and five minutes' presentation.
Invite discussion, but set a time limit.

Action 3.—Distribute a duplicated sheet asking
participants to list their elected officials: U.S.
senators, U.S. representative, governor, mayor
(city or county-level leader), state senator,
state representative, city councilman (or equiva-
lent), chief of police, fire chief. Ask participants to place an *X* by the name of each person
for whom they prayed by name in the last
week. Tabulate the answers. Distribute a sheet
listing the correct names, addresses, and forms
of salutation (most dictionaries carry this
information) for each public official.

Action 4.—Provide postcards for participants to
write a promise of prayer support (not neces-
sarily political) for some public official.

SESSION 2

Chapter 4: Decisions: They Are Yours; Make Them

Action 1.—List on a chalkboard the elements of
decision-making: (1) commitment to Christ's
way of life, (2) sufficient information, (3)
proper timing, (4) wisdom (knowing the difference between good and best), (5) effect on
others, (6) long-range effect on the one choosing (Will it tie him down or offer a new kind
or type of freedom?).

Action 2.—Discuss the elements of decision-
making. Using a Bible concordance, list Bible
verses affecting each element.

Action 3.—Plan a role-play situation: a youth
considering a college; or, a family deciding
to buy (and go deeply in debt for) a self-
propelled recreation vehicle.

Chapter 5: The Bible and Your Responsibility
Action 1.—Take a survey of the number of Bibles
in each home. Give time for thought. Total and
average for the group. Note that Bibles have
been available for the common man to own
for only a little more than two hundred years.
Action 2.—Display some old Bibles, if available.
Action 3.—Ask the participants to help design
a personal discipline for reading the Bible
daily: (using the readings suggested in *Home
Life* or various quarterlies; (2) systems of
reading the whole Bible in a period of time
(such as that suggested by the American
Bible Society); (3) or divide the number of
pages in a copy of the Bible by the time period
selected to read it through (this will give the
number of pages to be read daily); (4) date
the end of the reading each day with pencil.
Suggest that the participants write (in pencil)
in the flyleaf of their personal Bible their commitment to the discipline of daily Bible reading.

**Chapter 6: Your Brother Is Your
Responsibility: Win Him**
Action 1.—Ask participants to divide into groups
of two and read to each other the tract "A Full
and Meaningful Life."
Action 2.—After reading the tract, ask participants to share personal testimonies on the
theme, "When God became more than a word
to me," or "The person who introduced me to
Jesus."
Action 3.—Close the session by encouraging the
participants to write (in pencil) in the flyleaf
of their personal Bible names of two persons
with whom they will share "A Full and Meaningful Life." Ask them to do this before the

131

next Lord's Day services. Close with a prayer
of dedication.

Before the Next Session.—Ask participants to
keep a record of how they spent one day in
their lives. This will be used in session 3.

SESSION 3

Chapter 7: Your Influence: Guard It
Action 1.—Invite the participants to brainstorm
areas of bad influence Christians tend to overlook; such as, bad driving habits (ignoring
speed limits, expressing anger at other drivers),
explosive temper, insensitivity to others' feelings, misuse of income, inconsistency of life
at home and church, and gossip. Ask someone
to list the areas on the chalkboard.
Action 2.—Ask the participants to discuss the
implications of Jesus' statement in Matthew
28:18–20, "All power is given unto me in
heaven and in earth . . . and lo, I am with you
alway . . . ," as it relates to a Christian be-
coming a good influence in *all* of his life. (The
lordship of Christ and the presence of the Holy
Spirit in us give the strength and companion-
ship for decisions in righteousness and joy.)

**Chapter 8: Your Talents: You Can
Multiply Them**
Action 1.—With the group seated in a circle, ask
each participant to identify at least one of
God's potential or developed gifts to the second
person from his right. Give everyone a chance
to participate; then pray for one another.
Action 2.—Plan an extemporaneous reenactment
of the parable of the talents (Matt. 25:14–30),
beginning with the return of the landowner
(Matt. 25:19) and including the return of the

talents to him. Use four participants without practicing; however, let them use the Bible as they play their parts.

Chapter 9: Resources: Use Them Wisely

Action 1.—Distribute copies of the current or projected church budget. Divide into four groups. Ask each group to complete one of the following assignments and then report back.

(1) Figure the per-family gift needs to meet the budget; that is, if the budget is $100,000 and there are 200 families, the average per-family gift would be $500 per year. You will need to provide a close approximation of the number of church member families.

(2) Using the number of church member families, multiply that figure by 10 percent of the average family income in your area; that is, if there are 171 families and the average family income is $7800 per year, the potential tithe would be 171 times $780, or $133,380. For 200 families, it would be $156,000.

(3) Identify reasons why some church members will not give to the church. Share some answers to their objections; such as, "We are a fellowship of brothers in Christ," or "We can do far more together than apart."

(4) Discuss the balance or imbalance of the church's budget and methods of spending money.

Action 2.—Share the results of the records of the study of one day's time in the life of each participant. Was time wasted? Was everything done that was planned? Was the day typical? What can be done to recover the usefulness of time?

SESSION 4

Chapter 10: Sorrow: If You Have It, Handle It

Action 1.—Discuss the place of the church in helping Christians face sorrow. (A church is an equipping station, to aid life travelers to face life's decisions, sorrows, and joys in a victorious way. Every experience of sorrow can help a Christian grow stronger, teach him about God's love, and communicate some love to him. The Christian should pray for the sensitivity to search for God's answers in the "still small voices" of sorrow.) What can a church do to help in understanding and accepting sorrow?

Action 2.—Ask a participant to research and report on the effect of having no will in your state. Discuss the question, Is it right to lessen in every way possible the effects of sorrow on your survivors? For information about wills and estates, write to the Stewardship Commission of the Southern Baptist Convention, the stewardship secretary in your state, or the Baptist Foundation in your state.

Action 3.—Brainstorm ways your church can minister to one experiencing sorrow in your community.

Chapter 11: Love: You Have It; Share It

Action 1.—Form five or six small groups to discuss the implications of the following passages for a Christian in your community: 1 John 2:3–6; 1 John 2:8–11; 1 John 4:7–13; 1 John 4:16–21; James 2:1–8; Colossians 1:8. After ten minutes, call for reports.

Action 2.—Ask the participants to list practical ways the church can express Christian love in their world.

Action 3.—Ask for expressions of love from the participants to one another. Say: Is there someone in this group to whom you have neglected to express appreciative love? Why not do it now? The teacher or leader might start by (honestly) saying: _____, I love you. You have meant so much to me. Wait for others, as many as wish, to make similar statements.

Chapter 12: What Your Church Expects from You

Action 1.—Divide into groups of threes. Assign to each group a paragraph of the church covenant. Use your church's covenant or the one printed in *Baptist Hymnal*. Ask the groups to discuss their assignments and identify the difficulties some Christians have in honoring their portion of the covenant. Ask each group to state how they would lovingly seek to lead some Christian brother or sister back to the covenant commitment. After ten minutes for group work, call for reports.

Action 2.—Have intercessory prayer for those who have unwittingly let their influence become a detriment to the faith and for those whose covenant commitments seem a burden rather than a joy. Ask the participants to write in the flyleaf of their Bibles (in pencil) the names of two friends who are out of fellowship. Suggest a covenant of prayer among all participants for the persons they have privately listed.

Action 3.—Close the study with a circle of fellowship, holding hands and singing "Blest Be the Tie."

The Church Study Course

The Church Study Course that became effective January 1, 1970 consists of various types of short-term learning opportunities that meet the educational needs of Southern Baptists. It is a way to provide individual or group study in addition to curriculum offered on an ongoing basis.

The Church Study Course consists of courses to develop and train leaders and courses to help adults and youth grow toward maturity in Christian living. Units of instruction are provided for children and preschoolers to give them additional opportunities for foundational learnings.

The Church Study Course is promoted by the Sunday School Board, 127 Ninth Avenue, North, Nashville, Tennessee 37234, through the departments in the Church Services and Materials Division; by the Woman's Missionary Union, 600 North Twentieth Street, Birmingham, Alabama 35203; by the Brotherhood Commission, 1548 Poplar Avenue, Memphis, Tennessee 38104; and by the respective departments in the state conventions affiliated with the Southern Baptist Convention. Detailed information about the Church Study Course and the system of credits, diplomas, and record keeping is available from the agencies. Study course materials, supplementary learning aids, and forms for keeping records may be ordered from any Baptist Book Store.

Requirements for Credit

Adults and youth can earn study course credit through individual or group study.

INDIVIDUAL STUDY
1. *Individual experience.*—Reading, viewing, or listening to course material and completing the personal learning activities, companion workbook (study guide), or other requirements, for one to four credits, as specified.
2. *Reading.*—Reading, viewing, or listening to course material for one credit only.

GROUP STUDY
1. *Class experience.*—Group involvement with course material for the designated minimum number of class hours, for one to four credits, as specified.
2. *Lesson course study.*—Parallel use of designated study course material during the study of selected ongoing curriculum units, for one to four credits, as specified.
3. *Institutional study.*—Parallel use of designated study course material during regular courses at educational institutions, including Seminary Extension Department courses, for one to four credits, as specified.

No additional written work is required for a person in group study who participated in all class sessions and reads, views, or listens to the study course material. A class member who is absent from one or more sessions must complete the personal learning activities or other requirements for the material missed.

Teachers of study courses or of foundational units of instruction for children or preschoolers also are eligible to receive credit.

How to Request Credit for This Course

This resource is the required study material for course 3107 of subject area 31, Christian Growth and Service.

This course is designed for 7½ hours of Group Study in class and carries 3 credits. Credit also is allowed for use of this material in Individual Study, Lesson Course Study (if so designated), and Educational Institution Study. A person may receive Reading credit for this course.

After the course is completed, the teacher, the Church Training director, or a person designated by the church should complete Form 151 (Request for Course Credit) and send it to the Awards Office, 127 Ninth Avenue, North, Nashville, Tennessee 37234. Individuals also may request credit simply by writing the Awards Office.

When credit is issued to a person, the Awards Office sends two copies of the course credit slip to the church. The original copy should be filed in the person's record of training folder and the duplicate given to the individual. Accumulated credits are applied toward a diploma.

Writing a brief summary of each chapter qualifies a person for maximum credit in Individual Study. To receive credit, write a brief summary on a separate sheet of paper and fill in the request for credit form in this material. Cut out the form and give it and your summary sheet to a church leader or mail them in as directed.

INSTRUCTIONS: If requested by the teacher, fill in this form and give it to him when the course is completed. If preferred, mail this request for course credit to

AWARDS OFFICE
THE SUNDAY SCHOOL BOARD
127 NINTH AVENUE, NORTH
NASHVILLE, TENNESSEE 37234

Indicate Type of Study (✓)

☐ Institutional Study   ☐ Individual   ☐ Class   ☐ Lesson Course Study   ☐ Reading

State Convention	Association	Church Name		

Address of Church (Street, Route, or P.O. Box)	City	State	Zip

Mail to: (if different from church address)	Address (Street, Route, or P.O. Box)	City	State	Zip

Last Name	First Name	Middle	Mrs. (x)	COURSE TITLE	Course Code	Credit	Hours
				The Spirit-filled Steward	3107		

Cut along this line

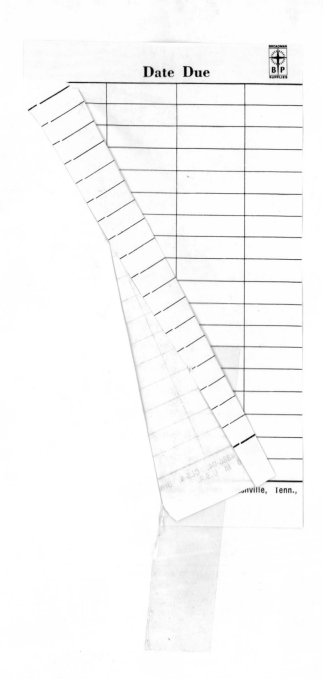

Date Due

...nville, Tenn.,